Literacy Plus

Language • Lifeskills • Civics

Joan Saslow

Consultants

Lisa Agao *California*	Robert Breitbard *Florida*	Virginia A. Cabasa-Hess *Illinois*	Janet S. Fischer *Massachusetts*	Carol Garcia *Illinois*
Glenda Gartman *California*	David L. Red *Virginia*	Lynn Reed *Arizona*	Margaret B. Silver *Missouri*	Gordon Thomas *Virginia*

Edwina Hoffman

Series Advisor

Longman

Literacy Plus A: Language, Lifeskills, Civics

Pearson Education, 10 Bank Street, White Plains, NY 10606

Vice president of instructional design: Allen Ascher
Senior acquisitions editor: Marian Wassner
Senior development editor: Jessica Miller-Smith
Vice president, director of design and production: Rhea Banker
Executive managing editor: Linda Moser
Senior production editor: Christine Lauricella
Production manager: Liza Pleva
Director of manufacturing: Patrice Fraccio
Senior manufacturing buyer: Dave Dickey
Cover design: Ann France
Cover photo credit (coins and bills): Corbis Stock Market
Text design and composition: Kim Teixeira and Wendy Wolf
Illustrations: John Amoss, pp. 2, 31, 45, 49, 57, 67, 71, 72, 75, 93, 144, 171; Burmar Technical Corporation, pp. 2, 4, 5, 27, 30, 33, 34, 37, 39, 51, 59, 122, 136, 138, 153, 154, 159, 161; Seitu Hayden, pp. 22, 40, 58, 71, 72, 90, 162, 184; Len Shalansky, pp. 17, 35, 53, 122, 132, 143, 158, 172, 175; Tom Sperling, pp. 1, 4, 6, 18, 24, 27, 32, 39, 46, 54, 75, 76, 78, 86, 93, 100, 111, 114, 117, 125, 129, 140, 144, 150, 157, 164, 165, 180, 186; Steve Sullivan, pp. 36, 39, 81, 82, 85, 90, 99, 103, 108, 112, 135, 139, 140, 147, 148, 152, 169, 179; Jill Wood, pp. 9, 10, 13, 14, 21, 31, 35, 36, 42, 45, 50, 52, 57, 60, 63, 64, 82, 85, 89, 94, 96, 103, 104, 107, 112, 118, 121, 126, 130, 133, 136, 137, 141, 147, 148, 153, 155, 159, 166, 168, 176, 183

Library of Congress Cataloging-in-Publication Data

Saslow, Joan M.
  Literacy plus: language, lifeskills, civics. Level A / Joan Saslow.
    p. cm.
ISBN 0-13-099610-6
1. English language--Textbooks for foreign speakers. 2. Life skills--Problems, exercises, etc. 3. Work--Problems, exercises, etc. I. Title.

PE1128 .S2748 2002
428.2'4--dc21   2002033988

3 4 5 6 7 8 9 10—RRD—07 06 05

LONGMAN ON THE **WEB**

Longman.com offers online resources for teachers and students. Access our Companion Websites, our online catalog, and our local offices around the world.

Visit us at **longman.com**.

What is *Literacy Plus*?

Literacy Plus: Language, Lifeskills, Civics is an adult course in English as a second language which starts at absolute beginner language and literacy level.

Learner profile

Written for adult immigrant learners, *Literacy Plus A* is for students who are preliterate in their own language and who know no English. Recognizing the reality that adults can't wait to become literate in order to work and carry on their lives, *Literacy Plus* offers instruction in survival English, basic literacy, and elemental civics concepts at the same time.

Unit structure

Within each of the 10 units, alternating pages are entitled "Literacy" or "Survival." In this way, students make daily progress on their pathway to literacy, communication, and mastery of the civics concepts that enable them to interact confidently with others in the American community and workplace. A tinted "Teacher" box at the bottom of each page clearly describes the goals and content of the page.

Learner placement and progress

Students may be placed in *Literacy Plus A* or *Literacy Plus B*, according to their level of preliteracy. Students who are preliterate in their native language should be placed in *Literacy Plus A*. When students have completed *Literacy Plus A*, they should then be placed in *Literacy Plus B*. Students who are literate in their own language, but not literate in English, may be placed directly into *Literacy Plus B*.

Components of the *Literacy Plus* course

- **Student's Book.** This 192-page, 10-unit student text contains daily lessons and practice in a convenient text-workbook format.
- **Audiocassettes.** A complete audio program contains listening and speaking practice of all vocabulary and conversations, as well as essential and effective listening comprehension exercises that prepare students to respond to authentic language outside of class.
- **Teacher's Edition.** A user-friendly wraparound edition contains daily lesson plans, teaching instructions, and complete tapescripts. Included in the Teacher's Edition is a CD-ROM with **Extra Practice Worksheets, Performance-based Achievement Tests,** and a **Placement Test**. These may be printed and duplicated as needed.
- **Flashcards.** These photocopiable cards allow group presentation, pair and group games, as well as reinforcement of vocabulary, conversation, and literacy skills. They are packaged with the Teacher's Edition.
- **Guide for Native-Language Tutors.** A short guide enables a native-language tutor or classroom aide to enrich the civics strand by featuring it in the student's native language.

Joan Saslow

Joan Saslow has taught English as a second language and English as a foreign language to adults and young adults in the United States and Chile. She taught workplace English at the General Motors auto assembly plant in Tarrytown, NY; and Adult ESL at Westchester Community College and at Marymount College in New York. In addition, Ms. Saslow taught English and French at the Binational Centers of Valparaíso and Viña del Mar, Chile, and the Catholic University of Valparaíso.

Ms. Saslow is the coauthor of *Workplace Plus: Living and Working in English*, a four-level adult ESL series. She is the series director of Longman's popular five-level adult course *True Colors, an EFL Course for Real Communication* and of *True Voices*, a five-level video course. She is also author of *English in Context: Reading Comprehension for Science and Technology*, a three-level series for English for special purposes. In addition, Ms. Saslow has been an editor of language teaching materials, a teacher trainer, and a frequent speaker at gatherings of ESL and EFL teachers for over thirty years.

Series advisor
Edwina Hoffman

Edwina Hoffman has taught English for speakers of other languages in South Florida and at the Miccosukee Tribe of Indians, and English as a foreign language in Venezuela. She provided teacher training in a seven-state area for federally funded multi-functional resource centers serving the southeastern part of the United States. Dr. Hoffman taught English composition at Florida International University and graduate ESOL methods at the University of Miami.

Dr. Hoffman is an instructional supervisor with the adult and vocational programs of Miami-Dade County Public Schools in Miami, Florida. She has acted as a consultant, reviewer, and author of adult ESOL materials for over twenty years. A graduate of Middlebury College, Dr. Hoffman's doctoral degree is from Florida International University.

Scope and sequence

Unit	Literacy	Survival Language	Civics Concepts	Vocabulary
1 page 7	• Recognize and trace triangle, circle, square. • Recognize left-to-right and top-to-bottom directionality.	• Make informal introductions. • Express and acknowledge thanks. • Give and accept a compliment. • Talk about first and last names. • Use titles Mr. and Ms. • Discuss occupations. • Ask about another's state of health and tell about one's own.	• Shake hands, exchange names, and express friendliness upon meeting someone new. • It's polite to express gratitude for a compliment. • Jobs are not determined by gender. • It's polite to ask about another's occupation. • It's polite to ask about another's health. It's important to say thanks when someone asks about your health.	• Occupations.
2 page 25	• Recognize numbers 1–30 as symbols that represent quantities as well as sequences.	• Ask for and give directions to a place. • Confirm information. • Offer help. • Ask for, state, and confirm telephone numbers. • Ask for and give zip code and area code.	• Wait on line to board a bus. • Park within the lines in a parking lot. • It's OK to ask a stranger for directions. • It's polite to offer assistance to a stranger. • It's OK to give a public official your phone number.	• Places in the community. • Types of housing.
3 page 43	• Trace and write numbers 1–10. • Recognize numbers on telephone key pad. • Recognize "0" as a number. • Recognize that the number system repeats in sets of 10. • Write the missing numbers on a grid from 1 to 50. • Recognize that buildings are numbered consecutively on alternating sides of the street. • Fill in missing building numbers on a neighborhood diagram.	• Ask for and give directions for public transportation. • Ask for walking or driving directions. • Report a fire or an accident to 911. • Ask someone to call. • Get a telephone number and area code from Directory Assistance.	• Public transportation is named and numbered. • In the U.S. emergency services are provided to the public. • 911 can help you in an emergency. • You can call 411 to get a phone number you need. • You can ask for directions over the phone.	• Means of transportation. • Emergencies and emergency vehicles.
4 page 61	• Recognize and trace capital E, F, T, I, L, A, H, Y, N, Z, K, X.	• Ask for and express location of items in a store. • Talk about clothes and sizes. • Apologize.	• It's OK to point at a place or a thing, though not at a person. • Expect to find prices on price tags. • Salespeople expect you to ask them where to find things. • Salespeople expect you to ask them to get you a size. • It's OK to tell a salesperson that something's wrong with merchandise or that it's too expensive.	• Types of stores. • Clothing. • Sizes.
5 page 79	• Recognize and trace capital M, W, V, U, J, S, C, O, G, Q, D, B, P, R.	• Exchange appropriate greetings and leave-takings. • Ask for and give the time. • Talk about work and school schedules. • Talk about arrival time at work. • Talk about business hours.	• It's polite to greet people with "Good morning," etc. • Work and school occur in regular schedules. • It's good to be on time. It's not good to be late. • Public offices and businesses keep regular hours.	• Times of day and clock times. • Days of the week. • Months of the year. • Places in the community.

Unit	Literacy	Survival Language	Civics Concepts	Vocabulary
6 page 97	• Understand concept that letters represent sounds. • Recognize sound-symbol correspondence of M, B, P, F, V, and H as initial sound of known words. • Trace first letter of known words.	• Ask for the location of foods. • Order in fast-food restaurant or cafeteria. • Order food items by size from a menu. • Talk about meals. • Politely express likes and dislikes. • Agree and disagree.	• Supermarkets are organized by categories. Salespeople can tell you where each food is. • It's expected that people's tastes vary. It's OK to compare tastes.	• Common foods and drinks. • Meals.
7 page 115	• Recognize that the alphabet has an "order" and that each letter has a name. • Recognize, read, and trace all lowercase letters. • Differentiate between upper and lowercase letters. • Write one's own name on a form, using capital and lowercase letters.	• Ask for and spell names. • State the age of another person. • Politely introduce people. • Provide marital status and spouse's name in an official setting. • Discuss national origin.	• Parents take their children to school in order to register them. The school will ask for the child's age. • It's friendly to ask where someone is from and to offer the same information about oneself. • It's OK to ask questions about a person's marital status. • It's OK to provide the names of people in one's family.	• Family and social relationships. • Marital status.
8 page 133	• Recognize sound-symbol correspondence of D, Z, S, T, N, and J as initial sound of known words. • Trace initial consonant of known words in both capital and lowercase letters.	• Report an injury. • Express concern. • Offer to get help. • Decline help. • Ask for and give directions. • Recognize common street signs. • Recognize basic safety signs and symbols. • Warn someone about a danger.	• You're expected to offer help to someone who is hurt or injured. • Signs protect your safety and that of others. Obey them. • The law requires safety restraints. You must obey the law.	• Parts of the body. • Places within buildings. • Directions within buildings. • Passenger restraints.
9 page 151	• Recognize sound-symbol correspondence of C, G, and K. • Read, say, listen to, and write dollar and cent amounts. • Recognize correct combinations of bills and coins to achieve a specified amount. • Recognize and discriminate between symbols as numbers, letters, words, or sentences.	• Recognize U.S. bills and coins and understand their monetary value. • Ask for change. • Pay for food. • Ask for prices. • Ask and answer questions about payment.	• It's OK to ask a stranger for change. • It's OK to ask salespeople for a price. • A sales tax is charged on many items. • Payment can be made with a variety of devices other than money. • It's OK to ask for a receipt. • Salespeople expect you to ask them about the products they sell.	• Coin and bill names. • Forms of payment.
10 page 169	• Recognize sound-symbol correspondence of L, Y, R, and W. • Recognize rhyming words, associate them with printed words, and read them. • Leave a space between words. • Leave a space between first and last names. • Demonstrate ability to write capital and lowercase letters on lines. • Write name, phone number, and area code on a form.	• Describe one's workskills. • Describe work experience in the U.S. • Provide information about past jobs and experience. • Provide references.	• Each workskill has a name. Speaking English is considered a workskill. • Potential employers ask about prior work experience. It's important to give correct information. • Ability to drive and to use machines and equipment is valuable in life and work. • It's important to bring references to a job interview.	• Workskills. • Occupations. • Machines, vehicles, and equipment.

🎧 **Look and listen.**

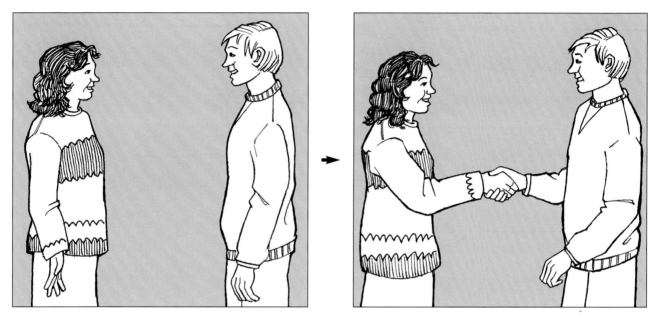

🎧 **Listen again and repeat.**

Pair work.

TEACHER

Survival: Introduce self with first name.
Civics concepts: Shake hands on greeting. Introduce yourself with your first name in an informal setting. Make eye contact.
New language: I'm [Maria]. / Nice to meet you [too].

Look.

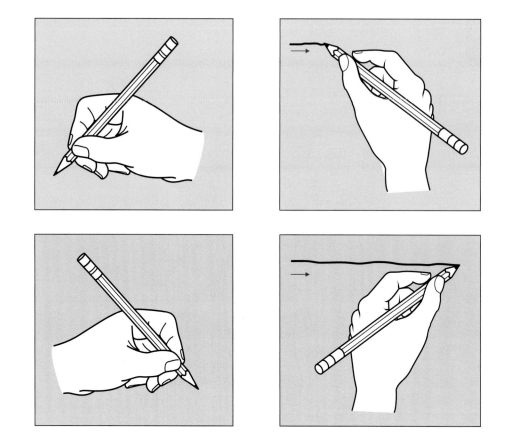

Trace.

→ ══════════════════════════

→ ══════════════════════════

🎧 **Look and listen.**

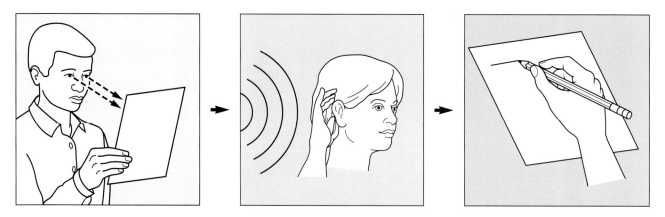

Trace.

TEACHER

Literacy: Practice tracing lines from left to right and top to bottom.
More practice: Units 1-3 (Student's Book), Worksheet 1 (Teacher's Edition CD-ROM).

Look.

Trace.

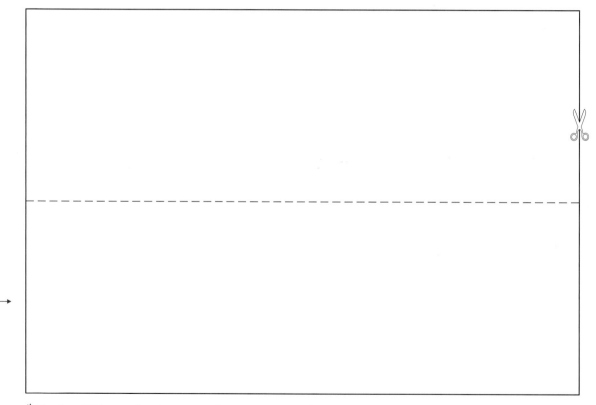

*—→

* Teacher: Write student's name in bottom portion of name tag.

TEACHER

Survival: Use first names in class. Understand concept that names are represented with written symbols. Trace own name.
More practice: Worksheet 2 (Teacher's Edition CD-ROM).

Circle.

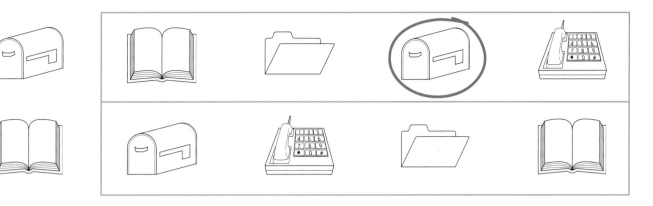

Cross out.

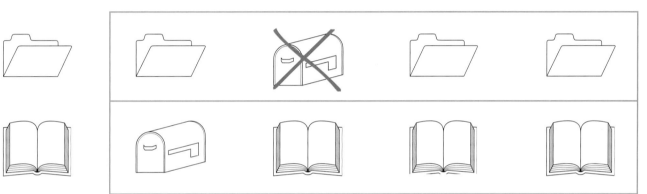

Trace.

→
→
→
→
→
→
→
→

TEACHER

Literacy: Copy circling, crossing out, and tracing lines from left to right.

🎧 **Look and listen.**

🎧 **Listen again and repeat.**

Pair work.

TEACHER

Survival: Say goodbye when departing another's company.
Civics concepts: Saying goodbye before leaving is good manners. It's OK to wave to say goodbye.
New language: Bye. / See you later.

NAME _____

Cross out.

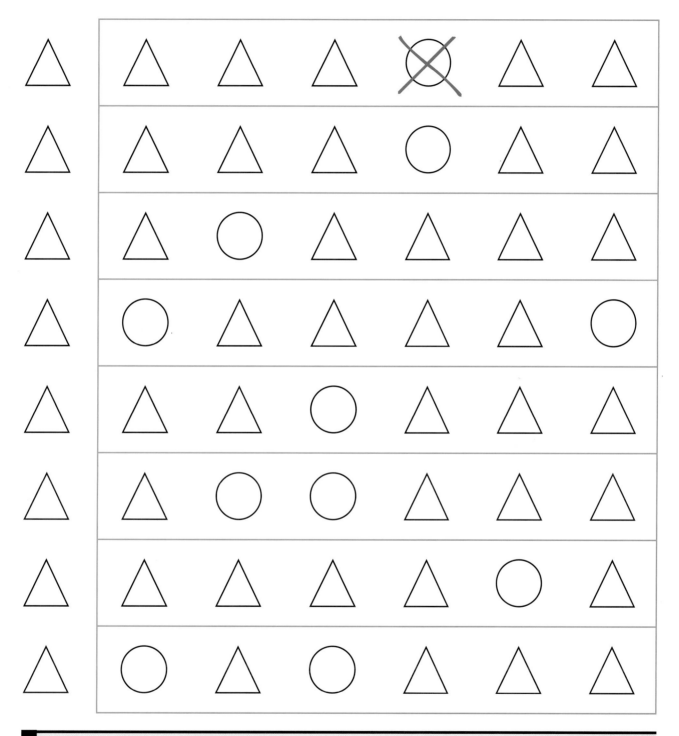

TEACHER

Literacy: Recognize triangle. Demonstrate recognition of difference in shapes.
More practice: Worksheet 3 (Teacher's Edition CD-ROM).

UNIT 1 • 7

Cross out.

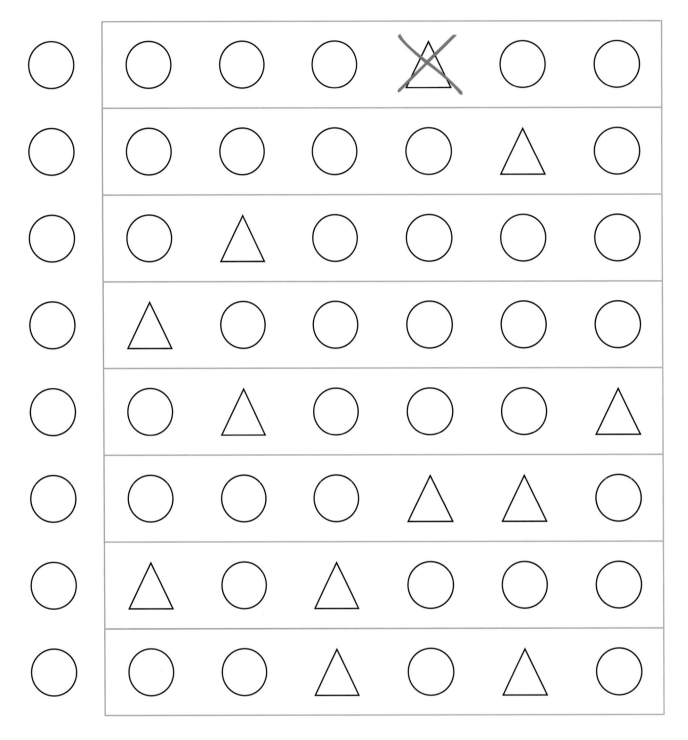

TEACHER

Literacy: Recognize circle. Demonstrate recognition of difference in shapes.
More practice: Worksheet 4 (Teacher's Edition CD-ROM).

🎧 **Look and listen.**

🎧 **Listen again and repeat.**

Pair work.

TEACHER

Survival: Introduce oneself in an informal setting.

Civics concepts: Shake hands, exchange names, and express friendliness upon meeting someone new. Use first names in informal settings.

New language: Hi. I'm [Nick].

🎧 **Look and listen.**

🎧 **Listen again and repeat.**

Pair work.

TEACHER

Survival: Ask about names. Express and acknowledge thanks.
Civics concept: Give first and last name in formal settings.
New language: What's your name? / Thank you. / You're welcome.

NAME _____

Cross out.

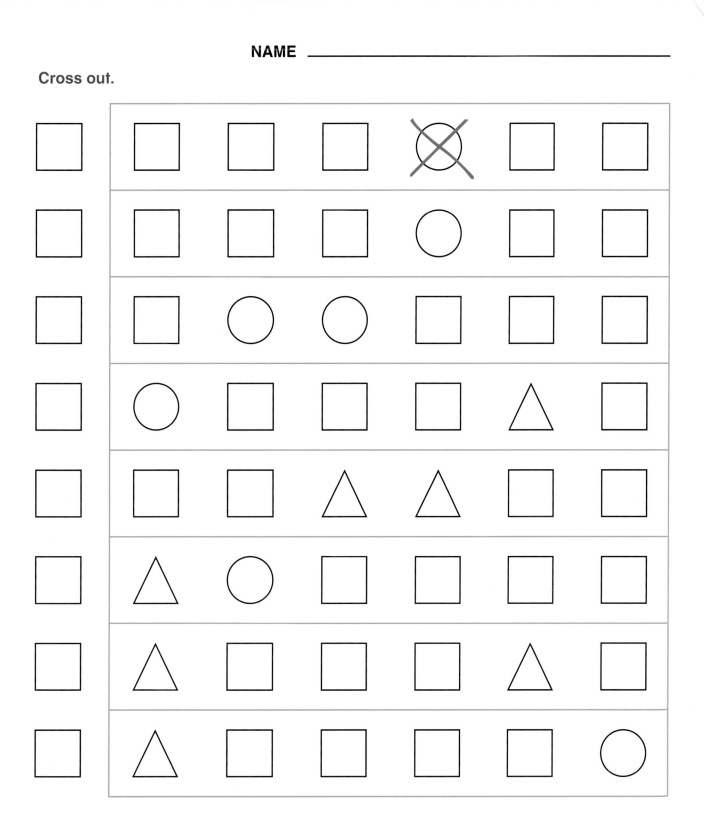

TEACHER

Literacy: Recognize square. Demonstrate recognition of difference in shapes.
More practice: Worksheet 5 (Teacher's Edition CD-ROM).

Circle.

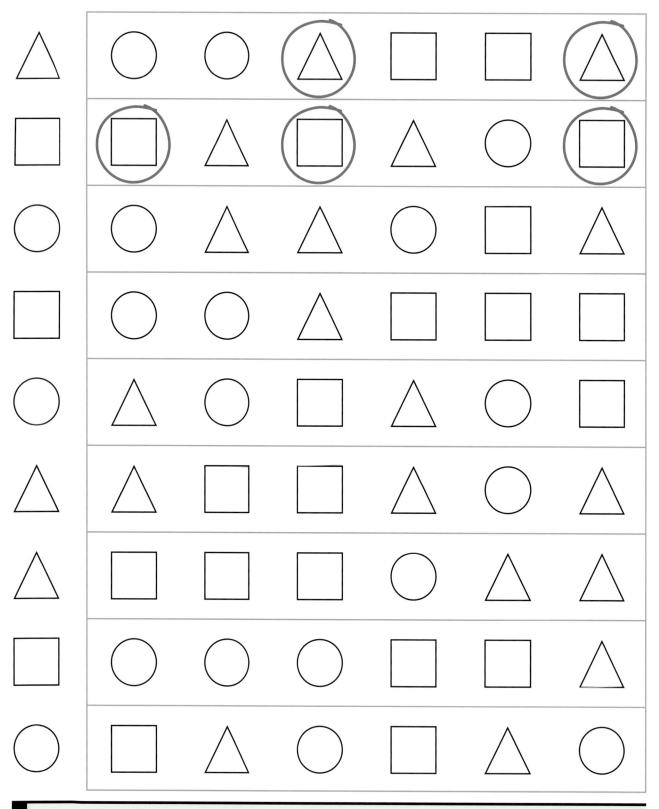

TEACHER

Literacy: Recognize triangle, square, and circle. Demonstrate recognition of sameness
in shapes.
More practice: Worksheet 6 (Teacher's Edition CD-ROM).

🎧 **Look and listen.**

🎧 **Listen again and repeat.**

Pair work.

TEACHER

Survival: Talk about last names. Give and accept a compliment.
Civics concept: It is polite to express gratitude for a compliment.
New language: What's your last name? / That's a nice name. / Thanks!

🎧 Look and listen.

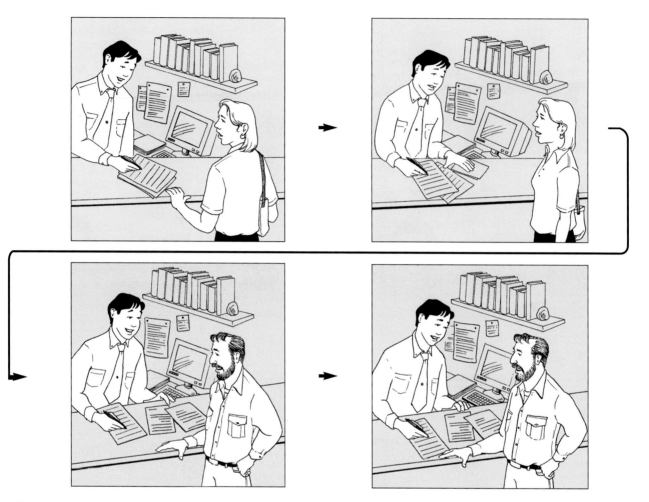

🎧 Listen again and repeat.

Pair work.

Trace.

Literacy: Observe and recognize left-to-right and top-to-bottom directionality. Trace a line from left to right and top to bottom.
More practice: Worksheet 7 (Teacher's Edition CD-ROM).

Trace.

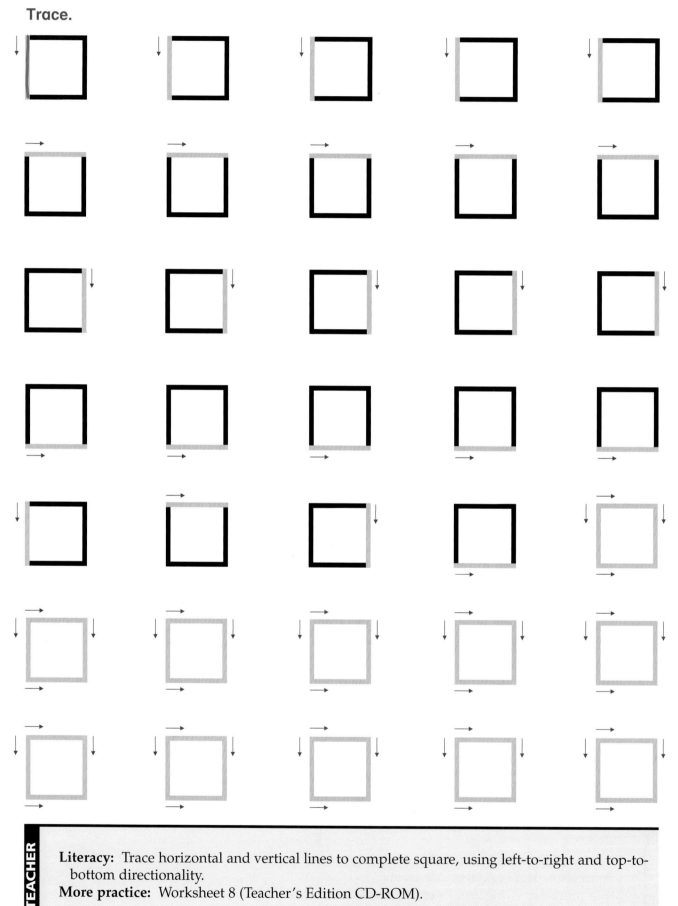

TEACHER

Literacy: Trace horizontal and vertical lines to complete square, using left-to-right and top-to-bottom directionality.
More practice: Worksheet 8 (Teacher's Edition CD-ROM).

🎧 **Look and listen.**

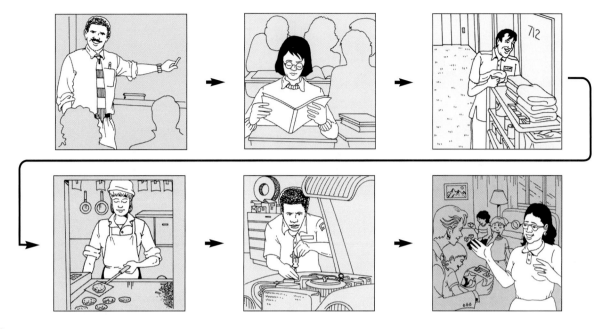

🎧 **Listen again and repeat.**

🎧 **Listen and circle.**

TEACHER

Survival: Learn names of occupations.
Civics concept: Jobs are not determined by gender.
New language: Teacher, student, housekeeper, cook, mechanic, babysitter.

🎧 **Look and listen.**

🎧 **Listen again and repeat.**

🎧 **Look and listen.**

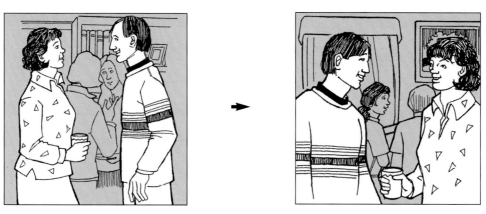

🎧 **Listen again and repeat.**

Pair work.

Trace.

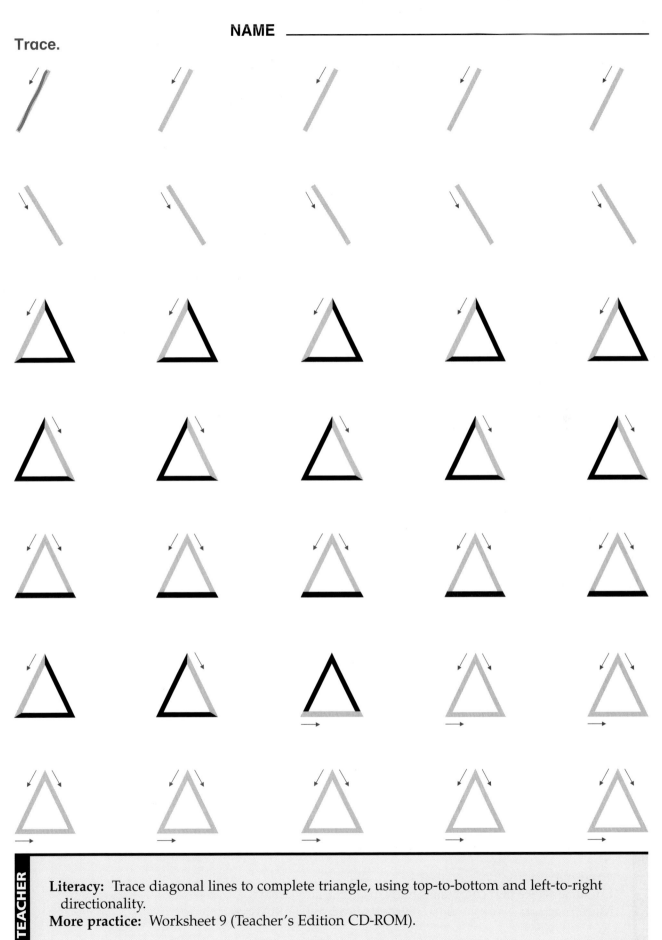

Literacy: Trace diagonal lines to complete triangle, using top-to-bottom and left-to-right directionality.

More practice: Worksheet 9 (Teacher's Edition CD-ROM).

Trace.

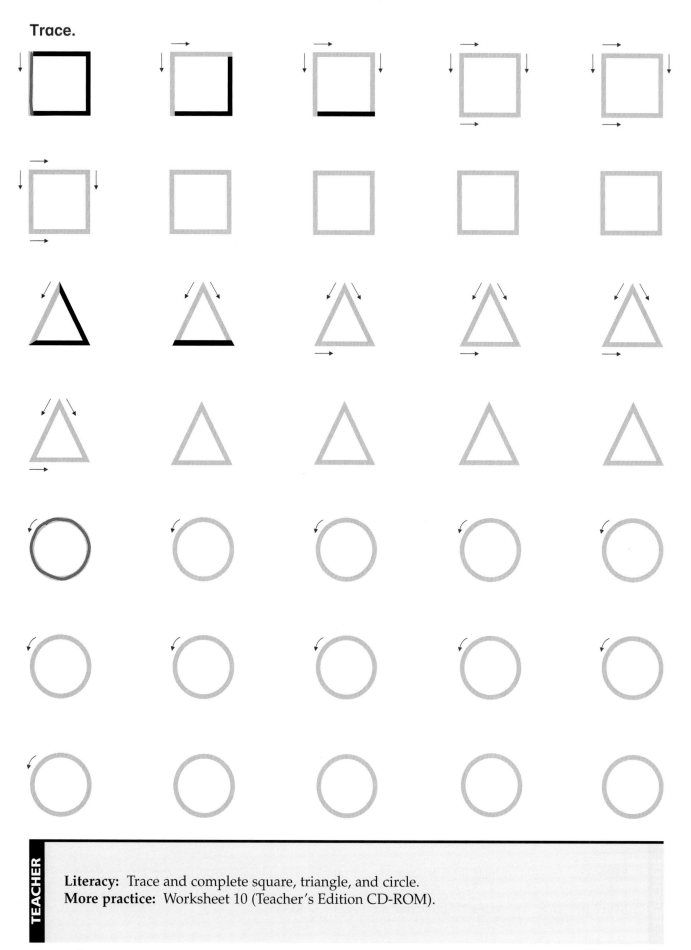

TEACHER

Literacy: Trace and complete square, triangle, and circle.
More practice: Worksheet 10 (Teacher's Edition CD-ROM).

20 • UNIT I

⌒ Look and listen.

⌒ Listen again and repeat.

Pair work.

TEACHER

Survival: Ask how someone is. Tell about oneself.
Civics concepts: It's polite to ask how someone is. It's important to say thanks when someone asks about your health.
New language: How are you? / [I'm] fine, thanks.

🎧 Look and listen.

🎧 Listen and circle.

🎧 Listen and respond.

 ➔  ➔

Trace.

Literacy review: Review left-to-right and top-to-bottom directionality. Trace square, triangle, circle.

More practice: Worksheet 11 (Teacher's Edition CD-ROM).

Literacy test: Teacher's Edition CD-ROM.

Talk about the pictures. Role-play conversations.

TEACHER

Survival / civics review: Point and name things in the pictures. Make statements about the pictures. Role-play conversations based on the pictures.
Tests: Teacher's Edition CD-ROM.

NAME _____

Circle.

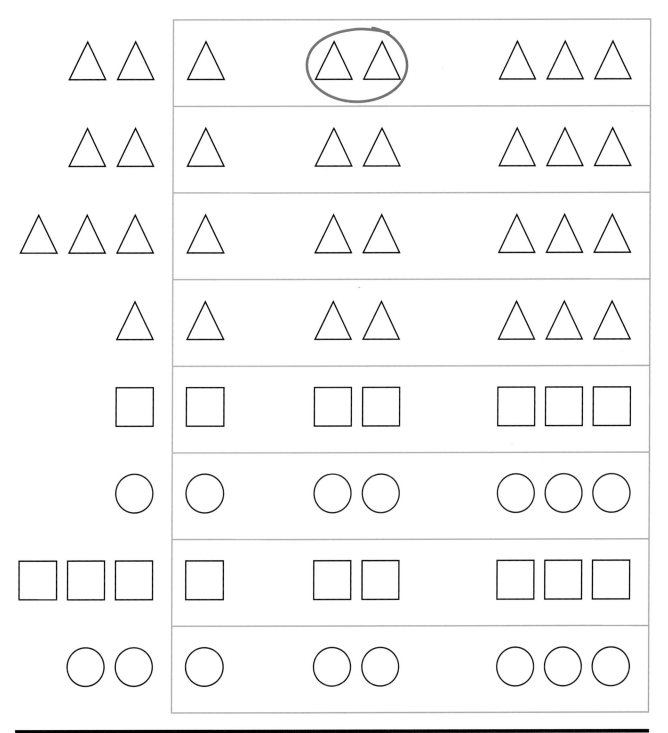

Literacy: Recognize sameness in quantity.
More practice: Worksheet 12 (Teacher's Edition CD-ROM).

TEACHER

🎧 **Look and listen.**

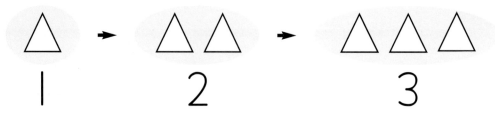

🎧 **Listen again and repeat.**

Circle.

○	①	2	3
▢▢▢	|	2	③
○○	|	2	3
△△△	|	2	3
▢▢	|	2	3
△△	|	2	3
○	|	2	3
○○○	|	2	3
△	|	2	3

TEACHER

Literacy: Understand that quantity can be represented by a symbol. Identify and understand meaning of numbers 1, 2, 3.
More practice: Worksheet 13 (Teacher's Edition CD-ROM).

🎧 **Look and listen.**

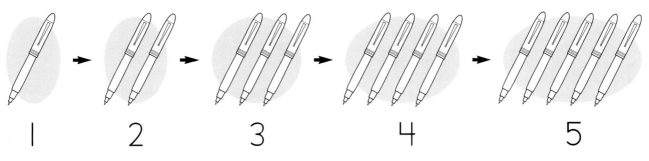

1   2   3   4   5

🎧 **Listen again and repeat.**

🎧 **Listen and circle.**

1	③
2	3
1	5
4	1
4	5

Pair work.

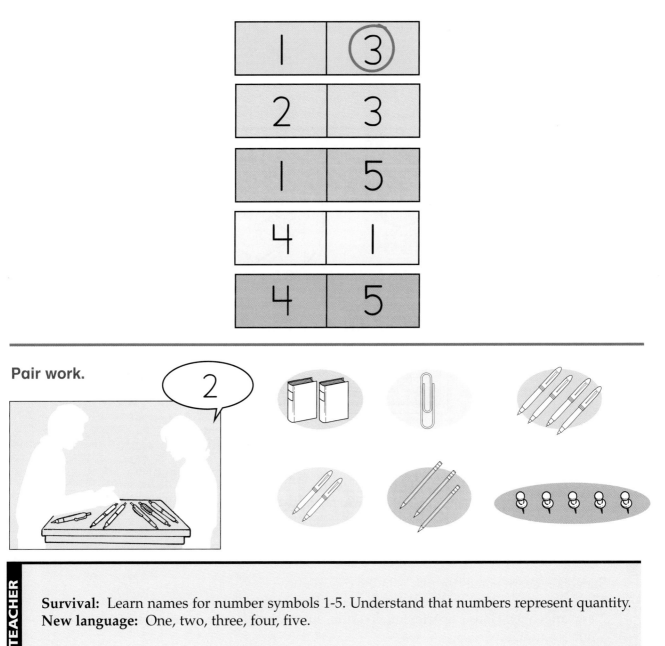

TEACHER

Survival: Learn names for number symbols 1-5. Understand that numbers represent quantity.
New language: One, two, three, four, five.

🎧 Look and listen.

🎧 Listen again and repeat.

🎧 Listen and circle.

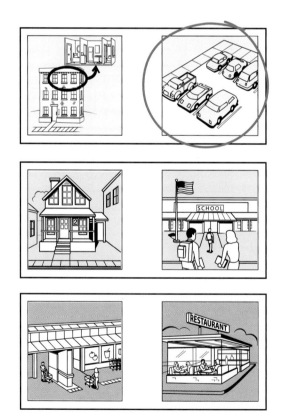

Circle.

1	①	2	5	4	3	①
2	2	1	3	4	5	2
3	4	5	3	2	3	1
4	3	4	4	5	4	2
5	4	4	5	1	3	2

🎧 **Look and listen.**

1	2	3	4	5

🎧 **Listen again and repeat.**

Circle.

	1	2	3	④	5
	1	2	3	4	5
	1	2	3	4	5
	1	2	3	4	5

TEACHER

Literacy: Recognize and differentiate numbers 1-5 as symbols. Associate quantity with number.
More practice: Worksheet 14 (Teacher's Edition CD-ROM).

🎧 **Look and listen.**

6   7   8   9   10

🎧 **Listen again and repeat.**

Circle.

6	9	⑥	7	⑥	9
9	8	10	6	9	9
7	6	8	7	10	7
10	9	10	6	10	7
8	8	7	8	6	9

Cross out.

9	9	9	✗	9	✗
8	8	6	8	10	8
6	9	6	9	6	6
10	8	10	10	7	10
7	9	7	7	7	6

Literacy: Recognize, understand, and differentiate numbers 6, 7, 8, 9, 10.
More practice: Worksheet 15 (Teacher's Edition CD-ROM).

🎧 Look and listen.

🎧 Listen again and repeat.

Pair work.

TEACHER

Survival: Ask for and give directions to a place. Confirm information.
Civics concepts: It's OK to ask a stranger for directions.
New language: Excuse me. / Where's the [school]? / It's on [Main Street]. / [Right] over there.

🎧 Look and listen.

🎧 Listen again and repeat.

Pair work.

TEACHER

Survival: Offer help. Ask for directions. Confirm information.
Civics concept: It's polite to offer assistance to a stranger.
New language: Can I help you? / Yes, please. / It's next to [the school].

Circle.

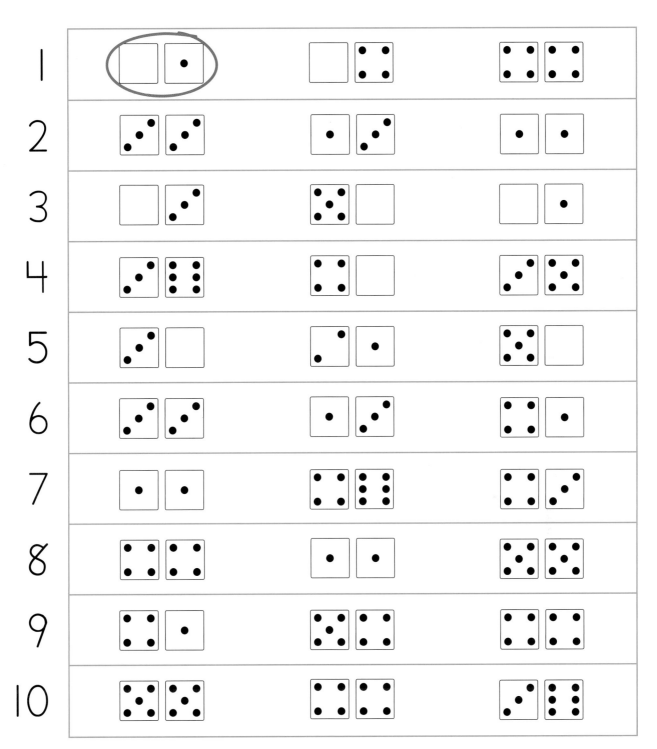

Literacy: Recognize and understand symbols 1–10. Understand that large numbers are made up of combinations of smaller numbers.
More practice: Worksheet 16 (Teacher's Edition CD-ROM).

TEACHER

🎧 Look and listen.

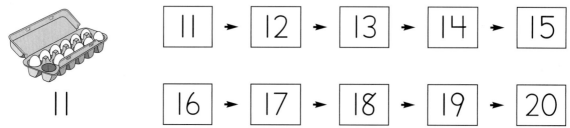

11 → 12 → 13 → 14 → 15

16 → 17 → 18 → 19 → 20

11

🎧 Listen again and repeat.

Cross out.

11	12	13	14	✗	15
12	10	13	14	15	16
13	14	15	18	16	17
14	15	5	16	17	18
15	16	17	18	19	10
1	2	3	4	7	5
2	3	13	4	5	6
3	4	5	10	6	7
4	5	6	7	18	8

TEACHER

Literacy: Recognize numbers 1-20 in sequence.
More practice: Worksheet 17 (Teacher's Edition CD-ROM).

🎧 Look and listen.

🎧 Listen again and repeat.

Pair work.

⌒ Look and listen.

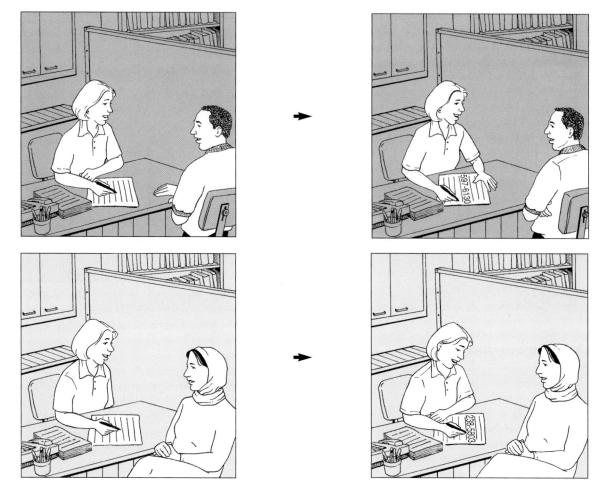

⌒ Listen again and repeat.

Pair work.

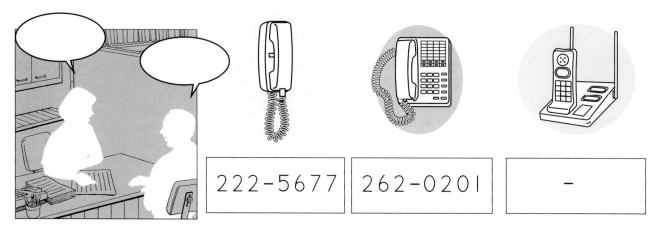

| 222-5677 | 262-0201 | — |

Survival: Ask for, state, and confirm telephone numbers.

Civics concepts: Telephones have numbers. It's OK to give a public official your phone number. Telephone numbers can be stated as individual digits.

New language: What's your telephone number? / [238-5803] / ["Oh" for "zero" in phone numbers].

🎧 **Look and listen.**

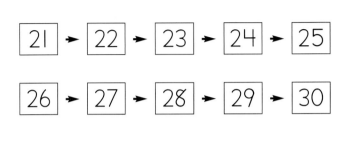

JUNE						
S	**M**	**T**	**W**	**T**	**F**	**S**
			1	2	3	4
5	6	7	8	9	10	11
12	13	14	15	16	17	18
19	20	21	22	23	24	25
26	27	28	29	30		

🎧 **Listen again and repeat.**

Circle.

♥♥ ♥♥ ♥♥ ♥♥ ♥♥ ♥	(21)	30
▫▫▫ ▫▫ ▫ ▫▫▫ ▫▫ ▫	16	22
○○ ○○ ○○ ○○ ○○ ○○ ○○ ○○ ○○	18	20
▲▲▲▲▲ ▲▲▲▲▲ ▲▲▲▲▲	30	15

TEACHER

Literacy: Recognize numbers 21-30 in sequence. Understand that items can be counted individually or in groups.
More practice: Worksheets 18–19 (Teacher's Edition CD-ROM).

Trace.

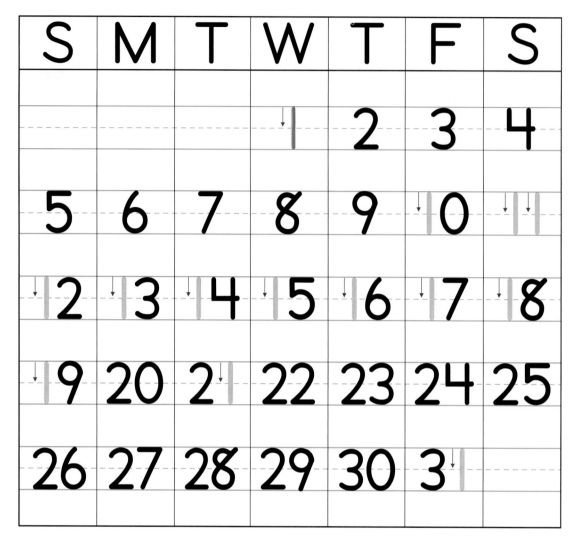

S	M	T	W	T	F	S
			1	2	3	4
5	6	7	8	9	10	11
12	13	14	15	16	17	18
19	20	21	22	23	24	25
26	27	28	29	30	31	

Literacy: Numbers indicate sequence as well as quantity. Trace numeral 1 and all 1s in numbers from 1 to 31, using top-to-bottom directionality.

🎧 Look and listen.

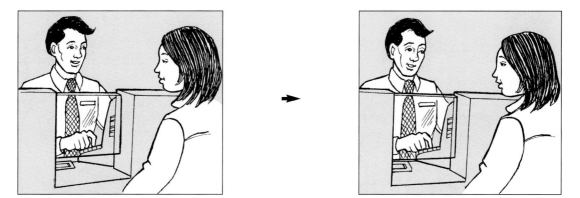

🎧 Listen again and repeat.

🎧 Look and listen.

🎧 Listen again and repeat.

Pair work.

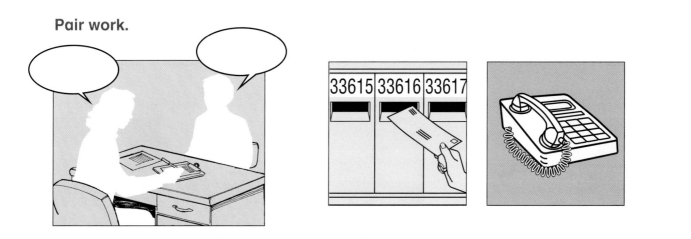

33615 33616 33617

🎧 **Look and listen.**

🎧 **Listen again. Circle the zip code.**

73142   78523

🎧 **Listen and respond.**

 ➡  ➡

Circle.

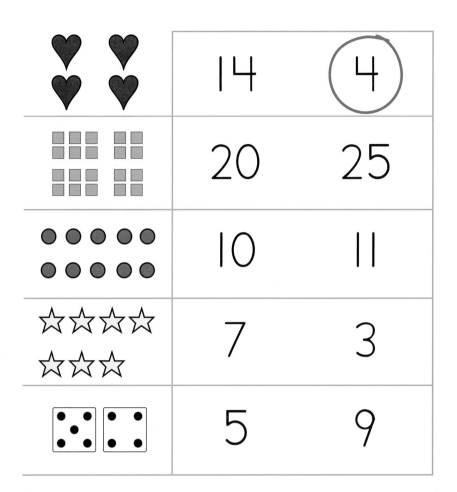

Cross out.

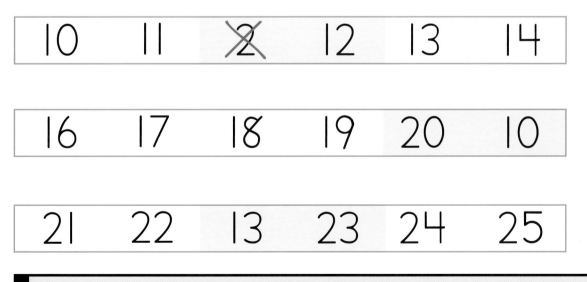

TEACHER

Literacy review: Numbers are symbols that represent quantity and sequence.
More practice: Worksheet 20 (Teacher's Edition CD-ROM).
Literacy test: Teacher's Edition CD-ROM.

Talk about the pictures. Role-play conversations.

TEACHER

Survival / civics review: Point and name things in the pictures. Make statements about the pictures. Role-play conversations based on the pictures.
Tests: Teacher's Edition CD-ROM.

42 • UNIT 2

Trace.

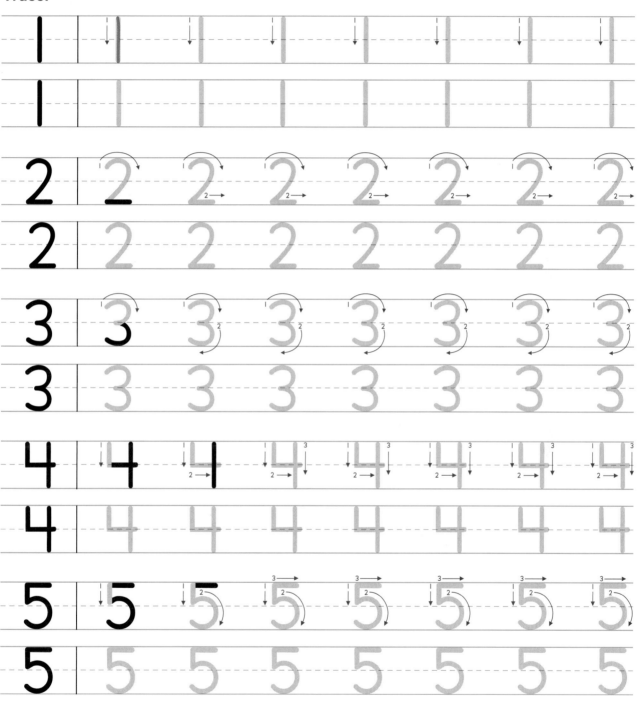

TEACHER

Literacy: Trace numbers 1-5, using top-to-bottom and left-to-right directionality in sequential strokes.
More practice: Worksheet 21 (Teacher's Edition CD-ROM).

Trace and write.

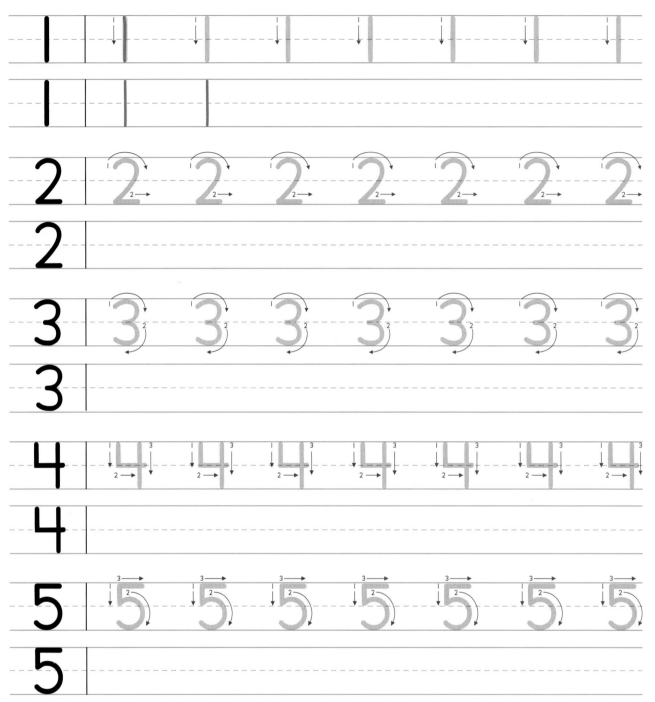

TEACHER

Literacy: Trace and write numbers 1-5 freehand, based on model and prior tracing practice.
More practice: Worksheet 22 (Teacher's Edition CD-ROM).

🎧 **Look and listen.**

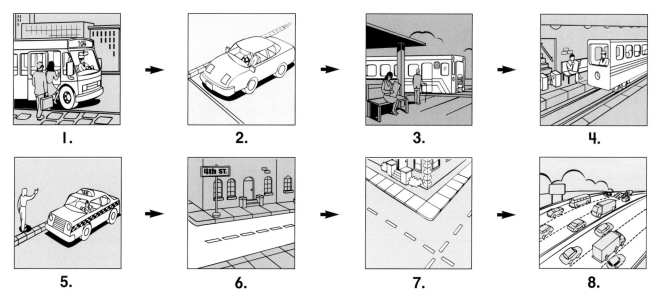

1.   2.   3.   4.

5.   6.   7.   8.

🎧 **Listen again and repeat.**

🎧 **Look and listen.**

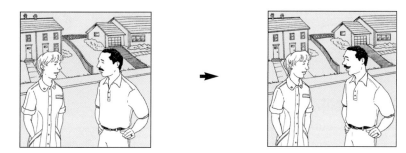

🎧 **Listen again and repeat.**

Pair work.

TEACHER

Survival: Learn means of transportation. Ask for and give directions for public transportation.
Civics concept: Public transportation is named and numbered.
New language: Bus, car, train, subway, taxi, street, corner, highway / How do I get to the [supermarket]? / Take the [bus]. / Which one? / The number [104].

🎧 **Look and listen.**

🎧 **Listen again and repeat.**

🎧 **Look and listen.**

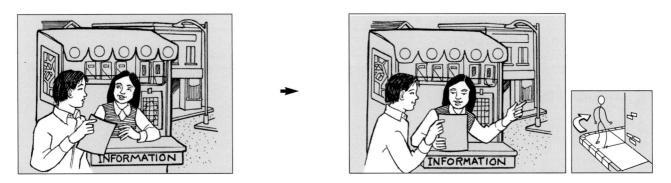

🎧 **Listen again and repeat.**

Pair work.

TEACHER

Survival: Ask for walking or driving directions.

Civics concepts: It's polite to be helpful to strangers. It's OK to ask strangers for help.

New language: Turn [right] at the corner. / I need directions. / Where are you going? / Here's the address.

Trace.

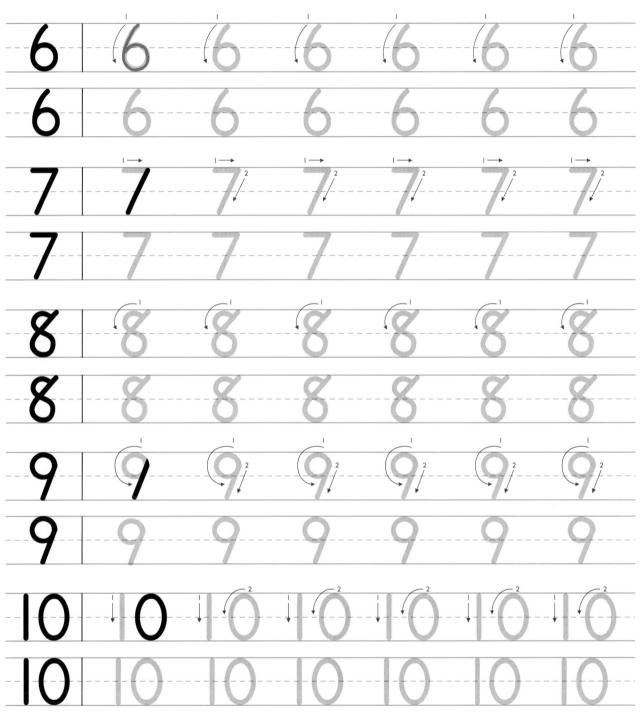

TEACHER

Literacy: Trace numbers 6-10, using top-to-bottom and left-to-right directionality in sequential strokes.
More practice: Worksheet 23 (Teacher's Edition CD-ROM).

UNIT 3 • 47

Trace and write.

6 6 6 6 6 6 6

6 6 6

7 7 7 7 7 7 7

7

8 8 8 8 8 8 8

8

9 9 9 9 9 9 9

9

10 10 10 10 10 10 10

10

TEACHER

Literacy: Trace and write numbers 6-10 freehand, based on model and prior tracing practice.
More practice: Worksheet 24 (Teacher's Edition CD-ROM).

🎧 **Look and listen.**

1.   2.   3.   4.

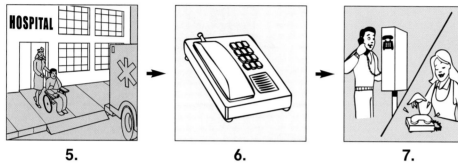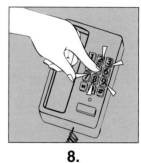

5.   6.   7.   8.

🎧 **Listen again and repeat.**

🎧 **Listen and circle.**

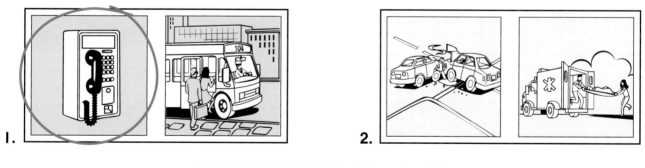

1.   2.

3.

🎧 Look and listen.

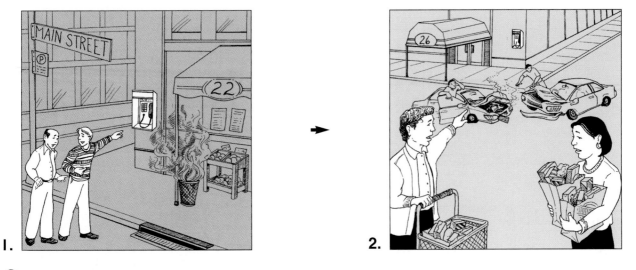

1. 　　　　2.

🎧 Listen again and repeat.

🎧 Look and listen.

🎧 Listen again and repeat.

Pair work.

Look.

Write.

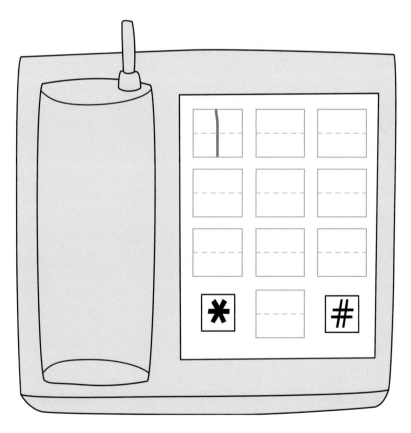

TEACHER

Literacy: Recognize numbers on telephone key pad. Recognize "0" as a number. Write numbers 0–9 on "buttons."
More practice: Worksheet 25 (Teacher's Edition CD-ROM).

🎧 **Listen and write.**

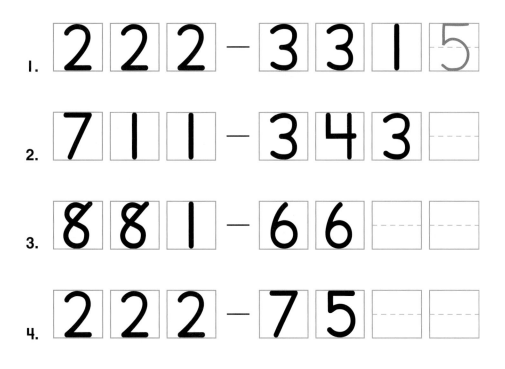

1. 2 2 2 - 3 3 1 5

2. 7 1 1 - 3 4 3

3. 8 8 1 - 6 6

4. 2 2 2 - 7 5

Pair work. Say a phone number. Write a phone number.

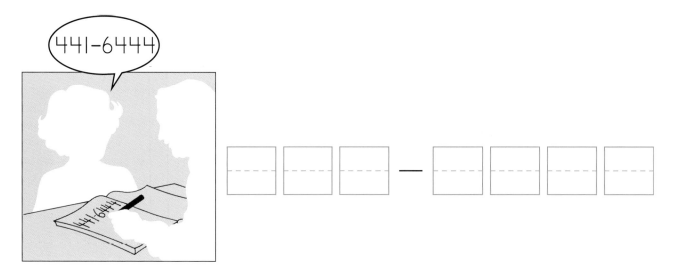

441-6444

TEACHER

Literacy: Write down phone numbers as if hearing them socially or from Information.
More practice: Worksheets 26–27 (Teacher's Edition CD-ROM).

🎧 Look and listen.

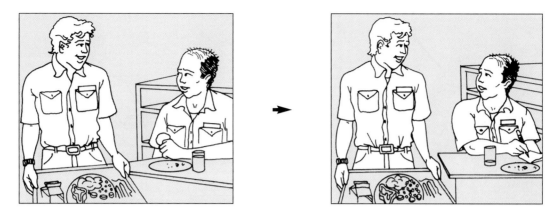

🎧 Listen again and repeat.

🎧 Look and listen.

🎧 Listen again and repeat.

Pair work.

599-3244   894-1234

450-3267   238-5803

🎧 **Look and listen.**

🎧 **Listen again and repeat.**

🎧 **Listen and circle.**

1. | (602) 555-4677 | (206) 555-4677 |

2. | (914) 555-0233 | (914) 555-0322 |

3. | (860) 555-7234 | (680) 555-7324 |

Trace.

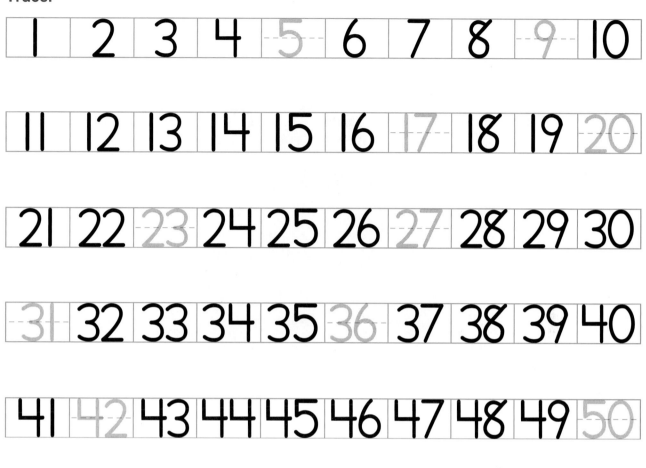

1 2 3 4 5 6 7 8 9 10

11 12 13 14 15 16 17 18 19 20

21 22 23 24 25 26 27 28 29 30

31 32 33 34 35 36 37 38 39 40

41 42 43 44 45 46 47 48 49 50

TEACHER

Literacy: Recognize that the number system repeats in sets of 10. Trace missing numbers from 1 to 50.
More practice: Worksheets 28–29 (Teacher's Edition CD-ROM).

Look.

Trace.

TEACHER

Literacy: Recognize that buildings are numbered consecutively on alternating sides of the street. Trace missing address numbers on a neighborhood diagram.
More practice: Worksheet 30 (Teacher's Edition CD-ROM).

⌒ Look and listen.

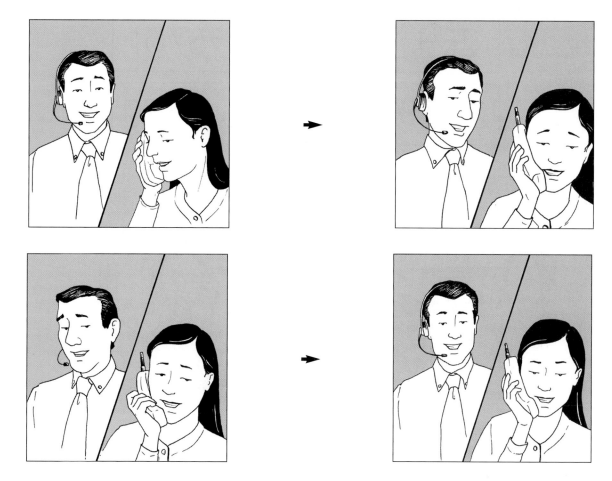

⌒ Listen again and repeat.

Pair work.

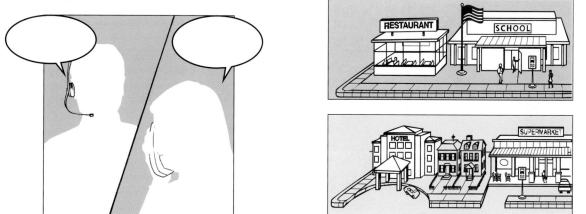

🎧 **Listen and circle.**

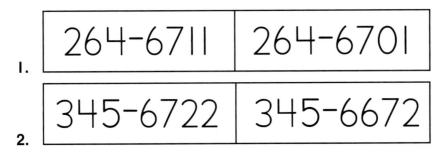

1. | 264-6711 | 264-6701 |

2. | 345-6722 | 345-6672 |

🎧 **Look and listen.**

🎧 **Listen and respond.**

1.　　　　　　　　2.　　　　　　　　3.

Trace and write.

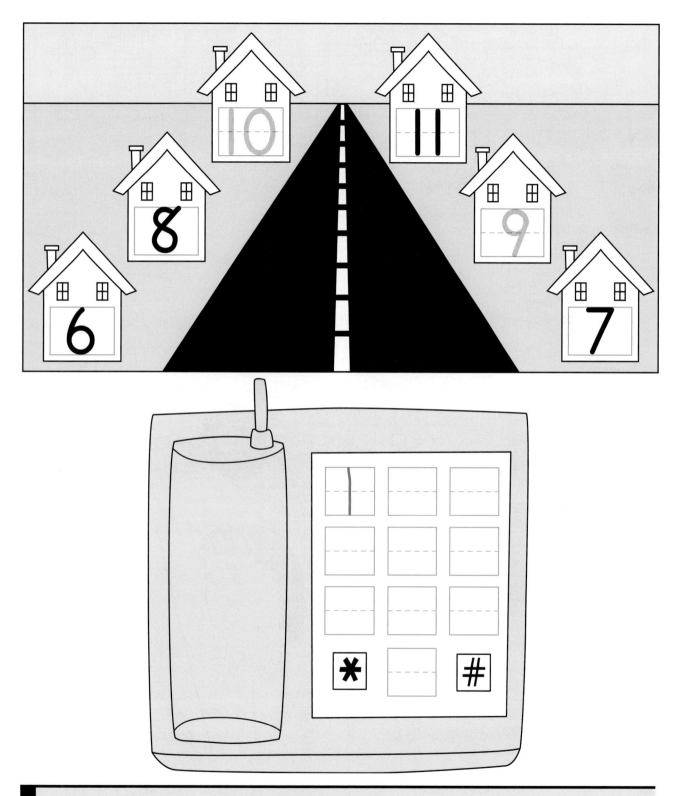

Literacy review: Review concepts of address numbers and telephone key pads. Fill in missing numbers.

More practice: Worksheet 31 (Teacher's Edition CD-ROM).

Literacy test: Teacher's Edition CD-ROM.

Talk about the pictures. Role-play conversations.

Survival / civics review: Point and name things in the pictures. Make statements about the pictures. Role-play conversations based on the pictures.

Tests: Teacher's Edition CD-ROM.

Cross out.

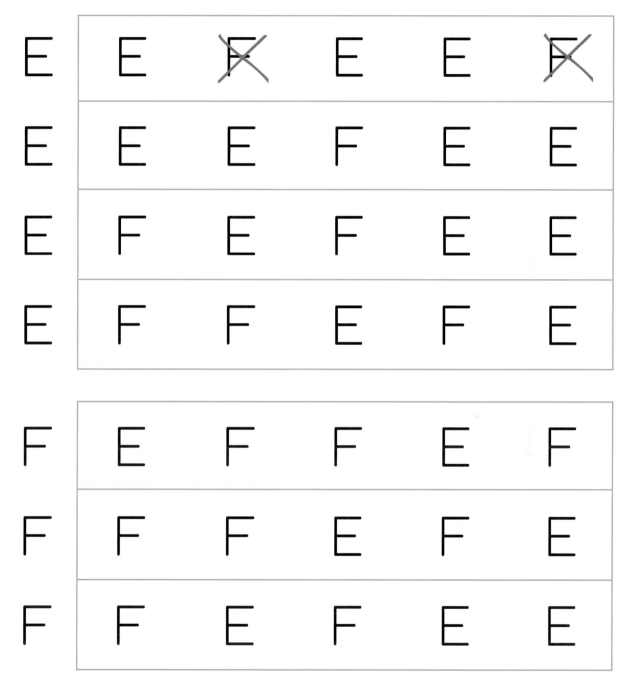

TEACHER

Literacy: Recognize capital E and F.
More practice: Worksheet 32 (Teacher's Edition CD-ROM).

UNIT 4 • 61

Trace.

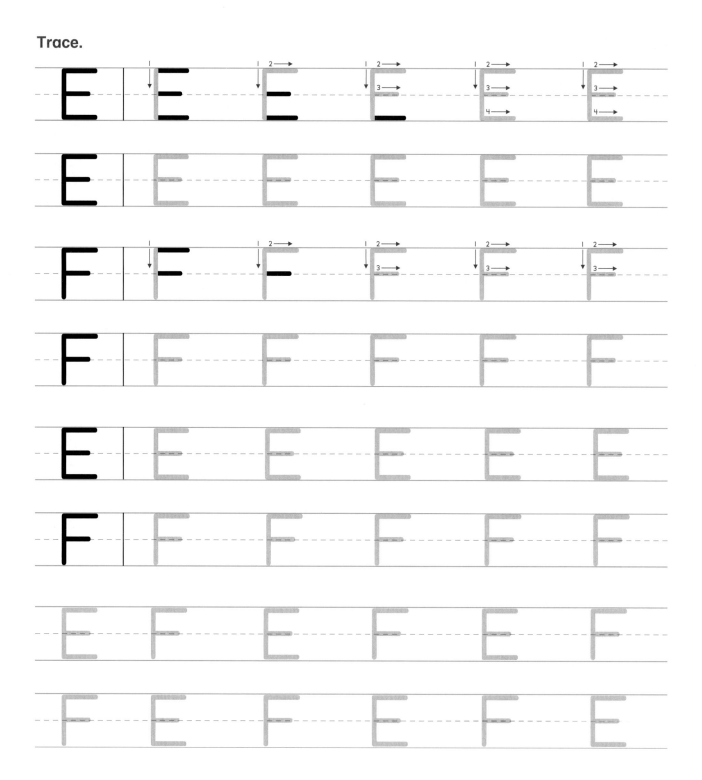

TEACHER

Literacy: Trace capital E and F, using classic uppercase penmanship.
More practice: Worksheet 33 (Teacher's Edition CD-ROM).

62 • UNIT 4

🎧 Look and listen.

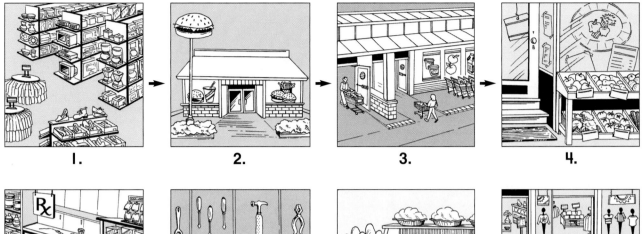

1.   2.   3.   4.

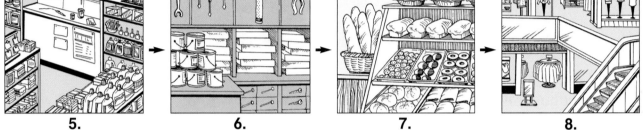

5.   6.   7.   8.

🎧 Listen again and repeat.

🎧 Listen and circle.

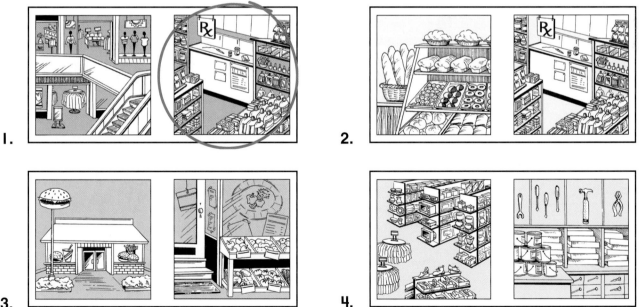

1.   2.

3.   4.

🎧 Look and listen.

1.   2.   3.

🎧 Listen again and repeat.

Pair work.

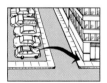

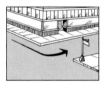

TEACHER

Survival: Ask for and give directions to places in the neighborhood.
Civics concept: It's OK to point at a place or a thing, though not at a person.
New language: Is there a [bakery] near here? / around the corner /
across from [the parking lot].

Circle.

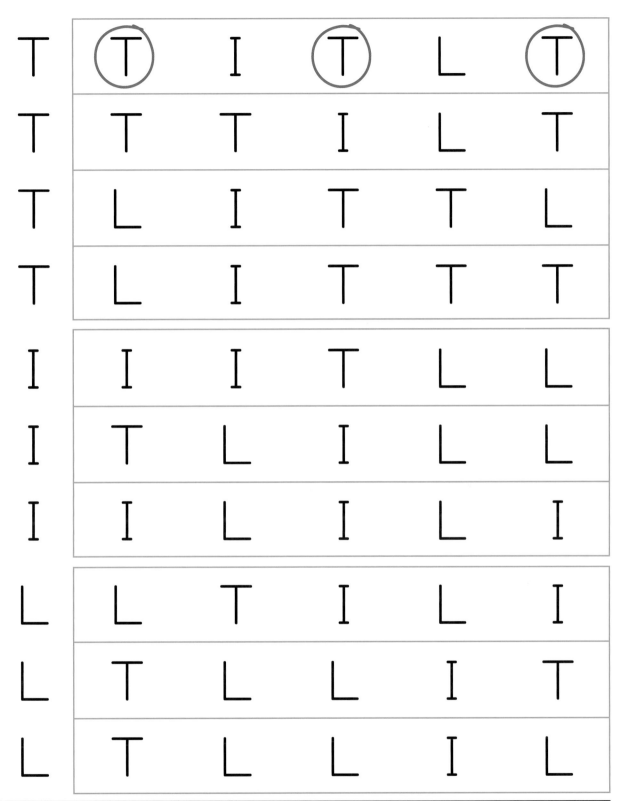

Literacy: Recognize capital T, I, and L.
More practice: Worksheet 34 (Teacher's Edition CD-ROM).

Trace.

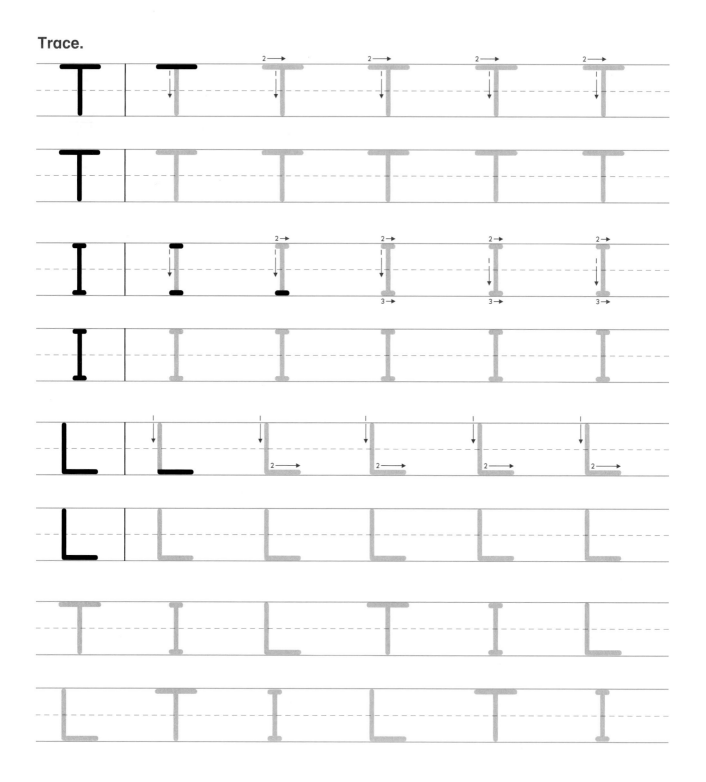

TEACHER

Literacy: Trace capital T, I, and L, using classic uppercase penmanship.
More practice: Worksheet 35 (Teacher's Edition CD-ROM).

66 • UNIT 4

🎧 **Look and listen.**

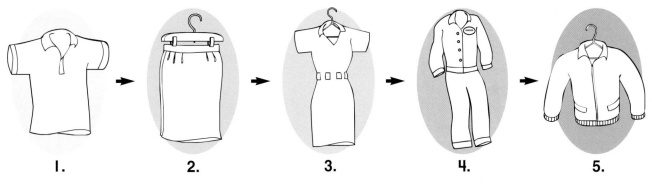

1.	2.	3.	4.	5.

🎧 **Listen again and repeat.**

🎧 **Look and listen.**

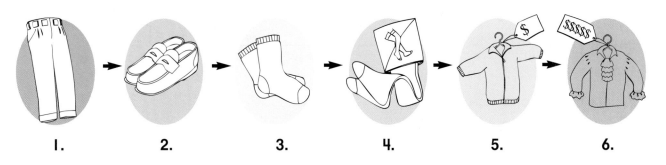

1.	2.	3.	4.	5.	6.

🎧 **Listen again and repeat.**

🎧 **Listen and circle.**

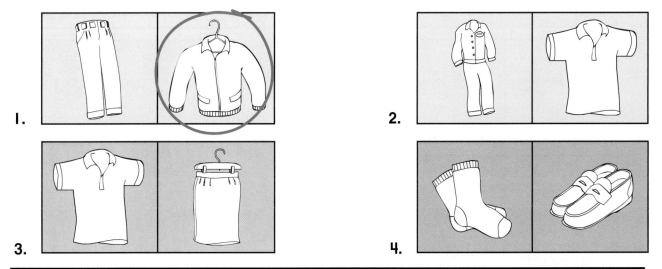

1.

2.

3.

4.

TEACHER

Survival: Learn vocabulary for types of clothing.
Civics concept: Look for prices on price tags.
New language: Shirt, skirt, dress, uniform, jacket, pants, shoes, socks, stockings, cheap, expensive.

🎧 Look and listen.

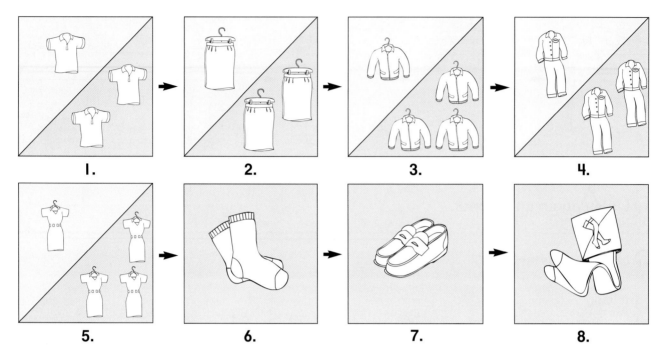

1.   2.   3.   4.

5.   6.   7.   8.

🎧 Listen again and repeat.

🎧 Listen and circle.

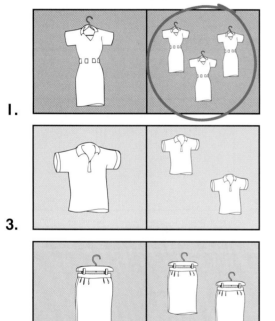

1.   2.

3.   4.

5.

Cross out.

Literacy: Recognize capital A, H, and Y.
More practice: Worksheet 36 (Teacher's Edition CD-ROM).

TEACHER

Trace.

TEACHER

Literacy: Trace A, H, and Y, using classic uppercase penmanhsip.
More practice: Worksheet 37 (Teacher's Edition CD-ROM).

🎧 **Look and listen.**

1.

2.

🎧 **Listen again and repeat.**

Pair work.

🎧 **Look and listen.**

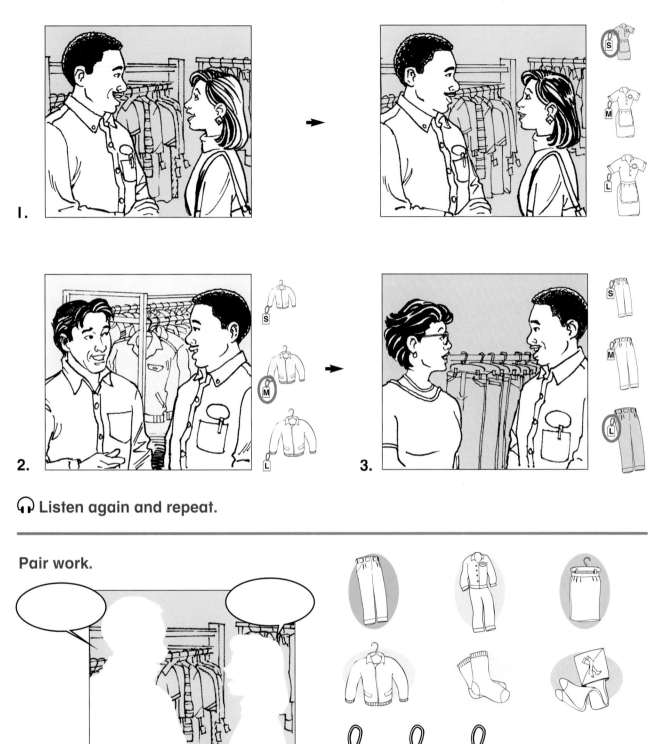

1.

2.

3.

🎧 **Listen again and repeat.**

Pair work.

S M L

Circle.

N	(N)	(N)	(N)	K	X
N	N	N	Z	Z	K
N	Z	X	K	N	Z
Z	Z	N	Z	N	K
Z	Z	N	Z	Z	K
K	K	K	Z	N	K
K	N	K	X	K	Z
X	K	X	Z	Y	X
X	X	X	X	K	X

Trace.

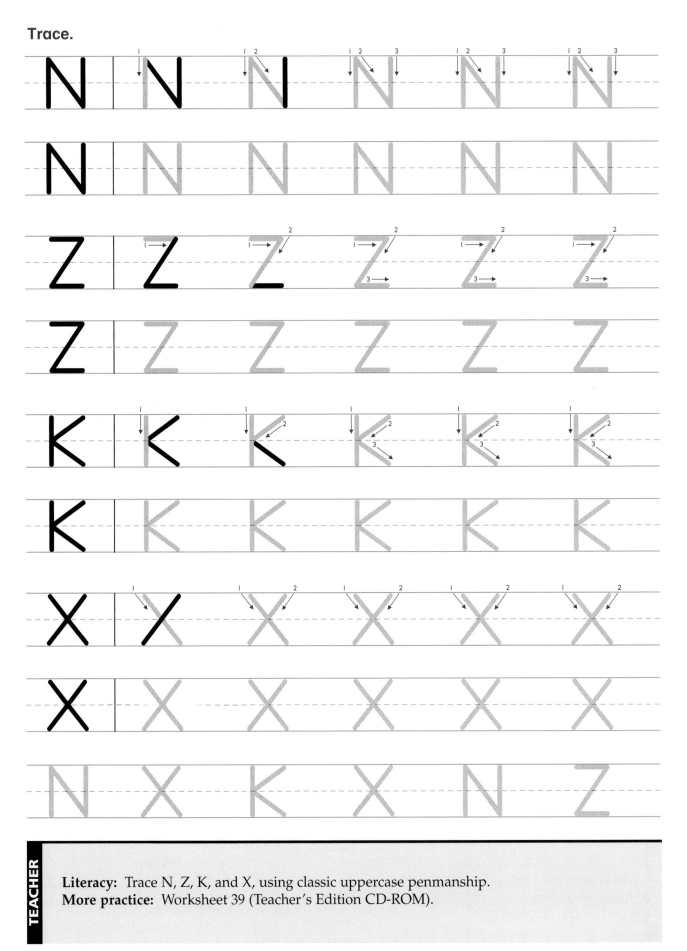

Literacy: Trace N, Z, K, and X, using classic uppercase penmanship.
More practice: Worksheet 39 (Teacher's Edition CD-ROM).

🎧 Look and listen.

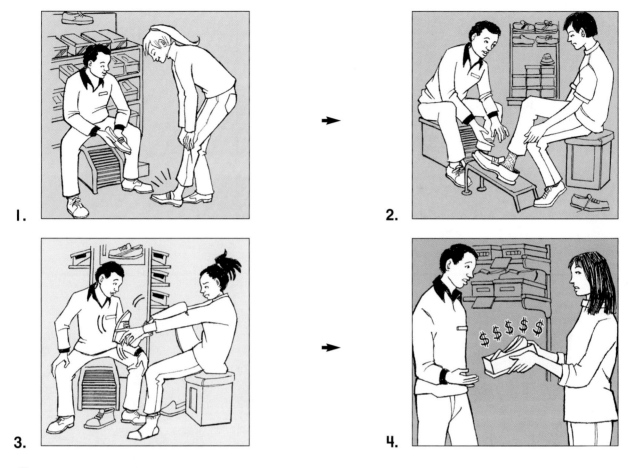

1.

2.

3.

4.

🎧 Listen again and repeat.

Pair work.

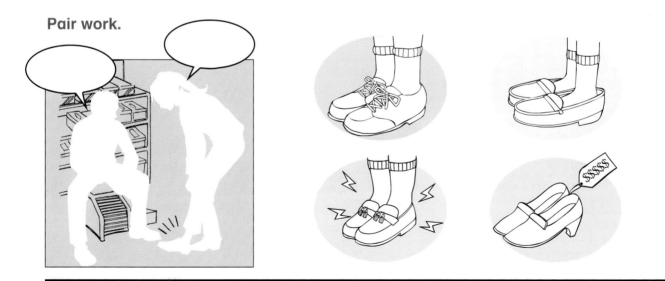

🎧 Listen and circle.

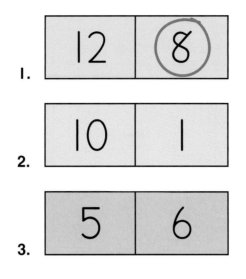

1. | 12 | (8) |

2. | 10 | 1 |

3. | 5 | 6 |

🎧 Look and listen.

🎧 Listen and respond.

1.　　　　　　　　　　　2.　　　　　　　　　　　3.

Circle and trace.

Z	M	K	Ⓩ	T	Y	Z Z
E	F	T	E	L	I	E E
F	E	F	T	H	L	F F
T	I	Y	T	H	F	T T
I	T	I	L	F	E	I I
L	I	T	F	H	L	L L
A	A	H	K	Y	N	A A
H	A	I	T	H	F	H H
Y	T	Y	I	N	X	Y Y
N	X	Z	A	N	Y	N N
Z	N	Z	L	A	X	Z Z
K	F	A	K	H	Y	K K
X	N	X	Y	A	K	X X

TEACHER

Literacy review: Recognize and trace capital E, F, T, I, L, A, H, Y, N, Z, K, and X.
More practice: Worksheet 40 (Teacher's Edition CD-ROM).
Literacy test: Teacher's Edition CD-ROM.

Talk about the pictures. Role-play conversations.

TEACHER

Survival / civics review: Point and name things in the pictures. Make statements about the pictures. Role-play conversations based on the pictures.
Tests: Teacher's Edition CD-ROM.

78 • UNIT 4

NAME _____

Circle.

M	(M)	(M)	W	N	(M)
M	M	W	Y	A	M
M	Z	M	W	M	N
M	W	M	M	V	M

W	M	V	W	W	M
W	Z	W	N	W	W
W	W	W	V	V	M

V	Y	V	A	W	K
V	V	V	V	Y	A
V	Z	X	V	N	V

Literacy: Recognize capital M, W, and V.
More practice: Worksheet 41 (Teacher's Edition CD-ROM).

Trace.

TEACHER

Literacy: Trace capital M, W, and V, using classic uppercase penmanship.
More practice: Worksheet 42 (Teacher's Edition CD-ROM).

80 • UNIT 5

🎧 **Look and listen.**

1.　　　　　　2.　　　　　　3.

🎧 **Listen again and repeat.**

🎧 **Listen and circle.**

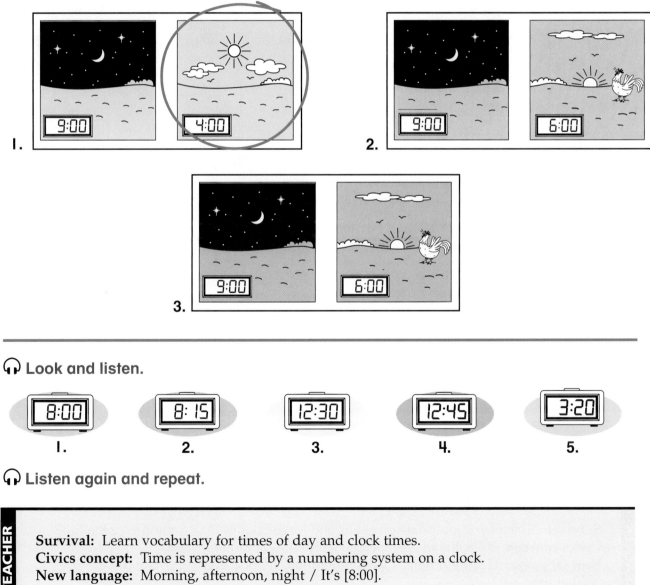

1.　　　　　　2.

3.

🎧 **Look and listen.**

8:00	8:15	12:30	12:45	3:20
1.	2.	3.	4.	5.

🎧 **Listen again and repeat.**

🎧 **Look and listen.**

1. `7:00`

2. `4:00`

3. `7:15`

4. `11:40`

🎧 **Listen again and repeat.**

Pair work.

`8:00` `10:15` `1:30` `9:35`

TEACHER

Survival: Exchange appropriate greetings and leave-takings. Ask for and give the time.
Civics concept: It's polite to greet people with "Good morning," etc.
New language: Good morning. / Good afternoon. / Good evening. / Good night. /
  What time is it?

Cross out.

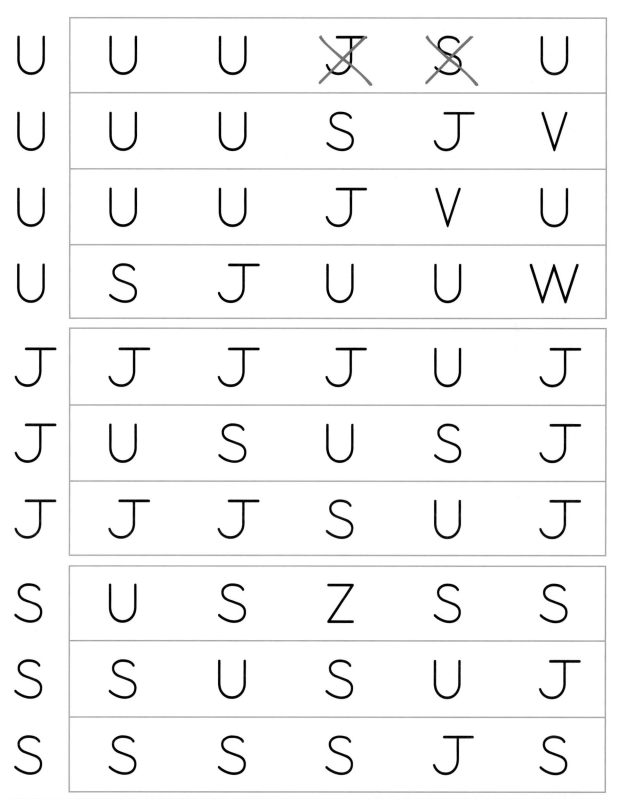

TEACHER

Literacy: Recognize capital U, J, and S.
More practice: Worksheet 43 (Teacher's Edition CD-ROM).

Trace.

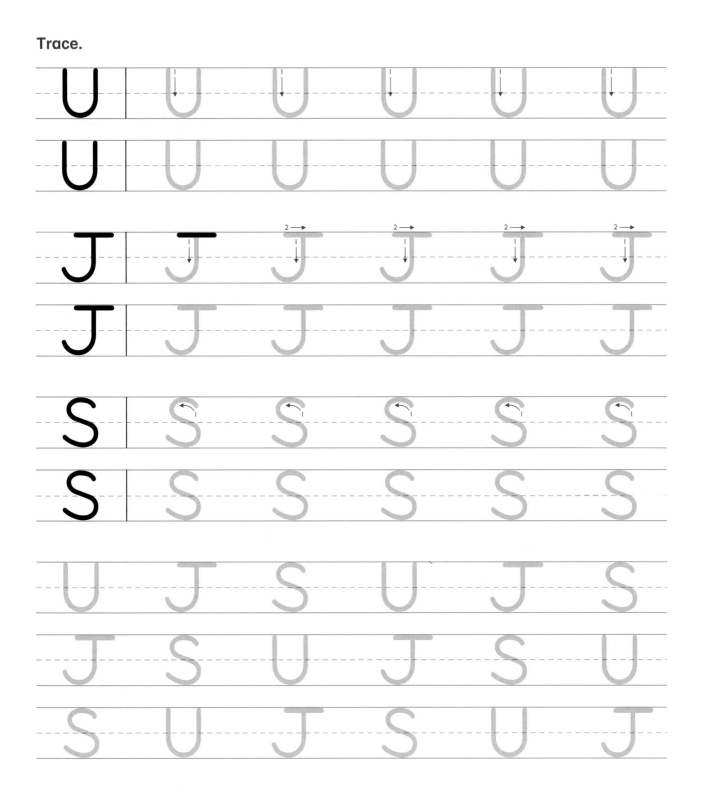

Literacy: Trace capital U, J, and S, using classic uppercase penmanship.
More practice: Worksheet 44 (Teacher's Edition CD-ROM).

🎧 **Look and listen.**

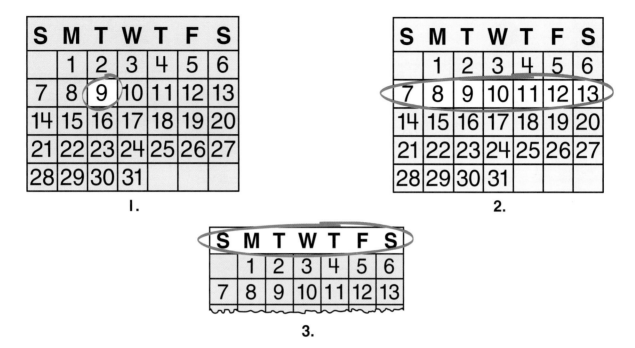

1.

2.

3.

🎧 **Listen again and repeat.**

🎧 **Look and listen.**

🎧 **Listen again and repeat.**

🎧 **Look and listen.**

I.   2.

🎧 **Listen again and repeat.**

🎧 **Look and listen.**

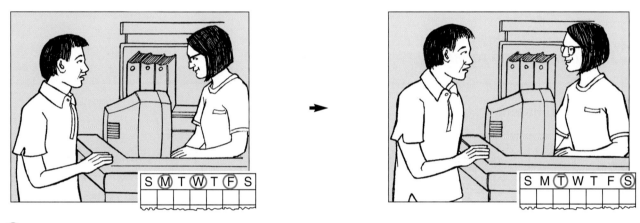

🎧 **Listen again and repeat.**

Pair work.

TEACHER

Survival: Talk about work and school schedules.
Civics concept: Work and school occur in regular schedules.
New language: When is [school/work]? / [School] is [Monday].

C | C | G̶ | C | G̶ | O̶

C | C | Q | O | C | G

C | G | C | O | C | C

O | O | C | O | C | O

O | O | C | O | G | Q

G | G | G | Q | C | G

G | O | C | O | G | O

Q | Q | G | C | Q | Q

Q | O | Q | C | Q | G

Literacy: Recognize capital C, O, G, and Q.
More practice: Worksheet 45 (Teacher's Edition CD-ROM).

Trace.

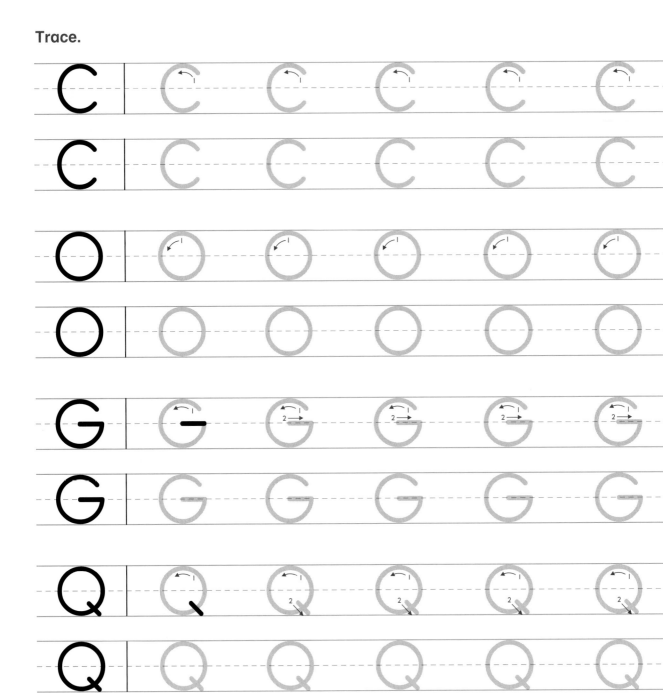

TEACHER

Literacy: Trace capital C, O, G, and Q, using classic uppercase penmanship.
More practice: Worksheet 46 (Teacher's Edition CD-ROM).

88 • UNIT 5

👂 Look and listen.

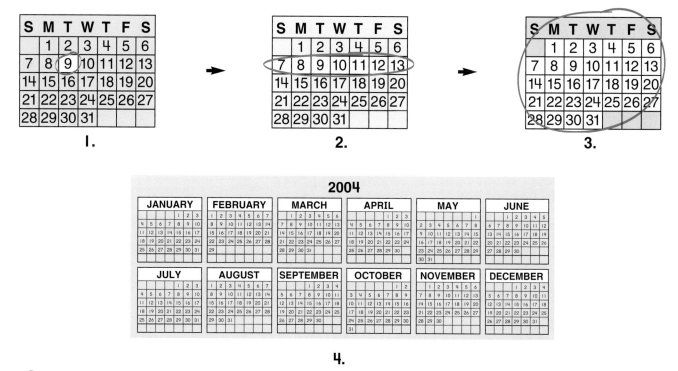

1.   2.   3.

2004

JANUARY	FEBRUARY	MARCH	APRIL	MAY	JUNE

JULY	AUGUST	SEPTEMBER	OCTOBER	NOVEMBER	DECEMBER

4.

👂 Listen again and repeat.

👂 Look and listen.

👂 Listen again and repeat.

🎧 Look and listen.

1.

2.

🎧 Listen again and repeat.

🎧 Look and listen.

1.   **2.**   **3.**

🎧 Listen again and repeat.

Pair work.

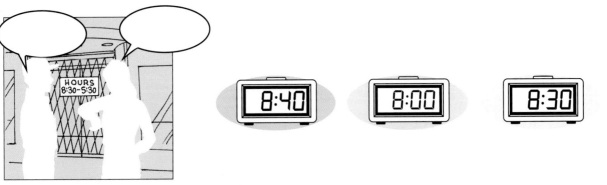

TEACHER

Survival: Talk about arrival time at work. Recognize importance of being on time.
Civics concepts: It's good to be on time. It's not good to be late.
New language: Early, on time, late / Oh good. / I'm [on time].
Sight word: Hours

Circle.

D	(D)	(D)	B	(D)	P
D	D	B	R	P	D
D	B	D	P	P	D
B	D	B	P	B	R
B	B	P	B	P	B
P	P	B	D	P	R
P	R	P	D	B	P
R	P	R	R	R	D
R	P	R	B	D	R

TEACHER

Literacy: Recognize capital D, B, P, and R.
More practice: Worksheet 47 (Teacher's Edition CD-ROM).

Trace.

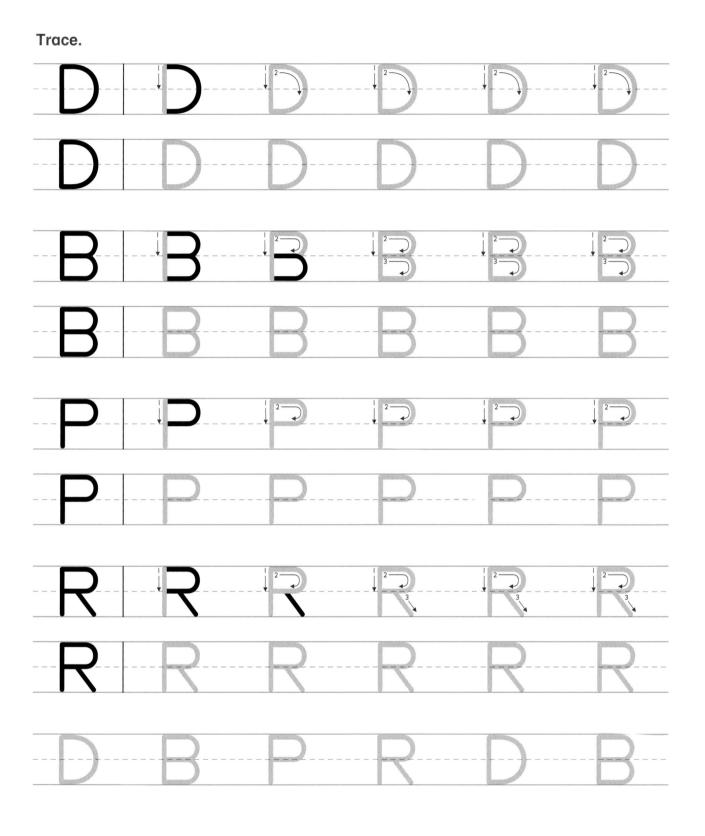

TEACHER

Literacy: Trace capital D, B, P, and R, using classic uppercase penmanship.
More practice: Worksheet 48 (Teacher's Edition CD-ROM).

92 • UNIT 5

Look and listen.

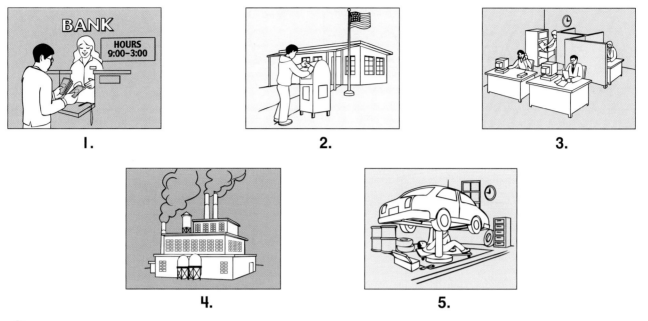

1. BANK — HOURS 9:00–3:00
2.
3.
4.
5.

Listen again and repeat.

Look and listen.

9:00-3:00   MONDAY-FRIDAY   SATURDAY SUNDAY

Listen again and repeat.

Pair work.

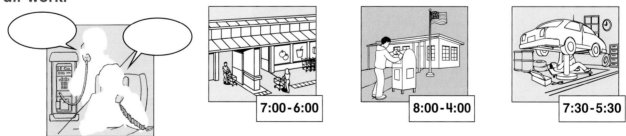

7:00-6:00   8:00-4:00   7:30-5:30

🎧 **Listen and circle.**

9:00 – 3:00	9:00 – 1:00

🎧 **Look and listen.**

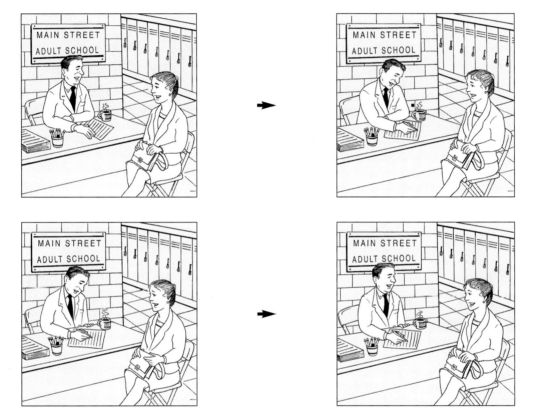

🎧 **Listen and respond.**

1.   2.   3.

Circle and trace.

M	(M)	W	Z	N	W	M	M
W	M	Z	W	A	V	W	W
V	A	Y	V	U	X	V	V
U	V	J	U	C	D	U	U
J	T	I	L	J	S	J	J
S	S	Z	C	U	J	S	S
C	D	U	J	C	S	C	C
O	O	G	Q	C	D	O	O
G	Q	O	C	D	G	G	G
Q	O	C	G	Q	D	Q	Q
D	C	B	P	O	D	D	D
B	B	D	P	E	R	B	B
P	D	B	P	R	F	P	P
R	K	P	R	A	B	R	R

TEACHER

Literacy review: Recognize and trace capital M, W, V, U, J, S, C, O, G, Q, D, B, P, R.
More practice: Worksheet 49 (Teacher's Edition CD-ROM).
Literacy test: Teacher's Edition CD-ROM.

Talk about the pictures. Role-play conversations.

Survival / civics review: Point and name things in the pictures. Make statements about the pictures. Role-play conversations based on the pictures.
Tests: Teacher's Edition CD-ROM.

NAME _____

Trace.

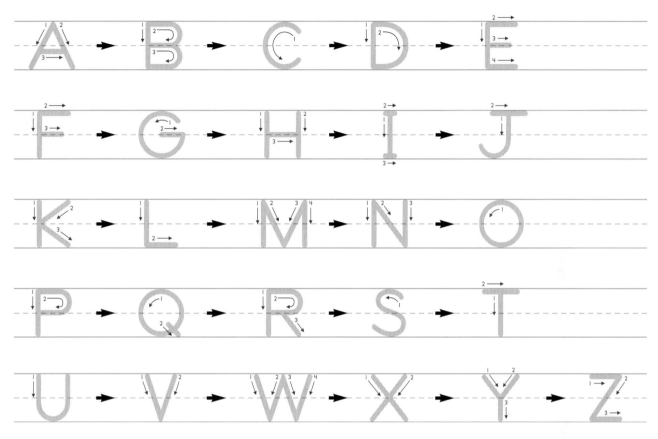

Literacy: Review tracing of capital letters in alphabetical order.
More practice: Worksheet 50 (Teacher's Edition CD-ROM).

TEACHER

UNIT 6 • 97

🎧 **Look and listen.**

M

🎧 **Listen again and repeat.**

🎧 **Look and listen.**

B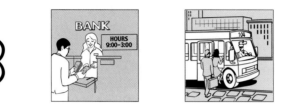

🎧 **Listen again and repeat.**

🎧 **Listen and repeat.**

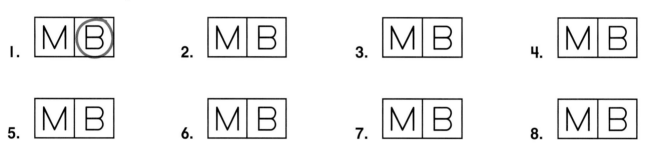

1. M (B)   2. M B   3. M B   4. M B

5. M B   6. M B   7. M B   8. M B

🎧 **Listen and circle M or B.**

TEACHER

Literacy: Begin to understand concept that letters represent sounds. Recognize sound-symbol correspondence of M and B as initial sound of known words.

🎧 **Look and listen.**

1. 2. 3. 4.

5. 6. 7. 8.

🎧 **Listen again and repeat.**

🎧 **Look and listen.**

1. 2. 3.

4. 5. 6.

🎧 **Listen again and repeat.**

🎧 **Listen and circle.**

1. 2. 3.

TEACHER

Survival: Learn names of a number of common foods and drinks.
New language: Chicken, meat, fish, cheese, bread, rice, pasta, fruit, milk, coffee, tea, juice, water, oil.

🎧 **Look and listen.**

1.

2.

🎧 **Listen again and repeat.**

Pair work.

TEACHER

Survival: Ask for the location of foods in a grocery or supermarket.

Civics concepts: Supermarkets are organized by categories. Salespeople can tell you where each food is.

New language: Aisle [2].

🎧 Look and listen.

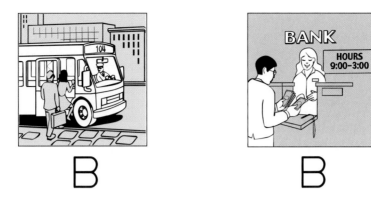

B   B

🎧 Listen again and repeat.

🎧 Look and listen.

M   M

🎧 Listen again and repeat.

🎧 Listen and repeat.

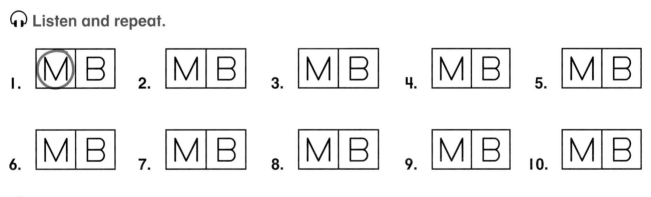

1. M B   2. M B   3. M B   4. M B   5. M B

6. M B   7. M B   8. M B   9. M B   10. M B

🎧 Listen and circle M or B.

TEACHER

Literacy: Discriminate between M and B as initial sound of known words.
Recognize M and B.

Say the word. Circle M or B.

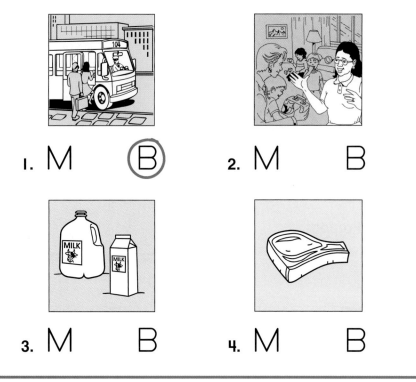

1. M (B)
2. M   B
3. M   B
4. M   B

Circle M and B.

M   (M)AY   MILK   MEAT

B   (B)US   BAKERY   BANK

TEACHER

Literacy: Discriminate between M and B as initial sound of known words.
More practice: Worksheet 51 (Teacher's Edition CD-ROM).

 **Look and listen.**

1.

2.

3.

4.

5.

6.

7.

Listen again and repeat.

Look and listen.

Listen again and repeat.

Pair work.

🎧 Look and listen.

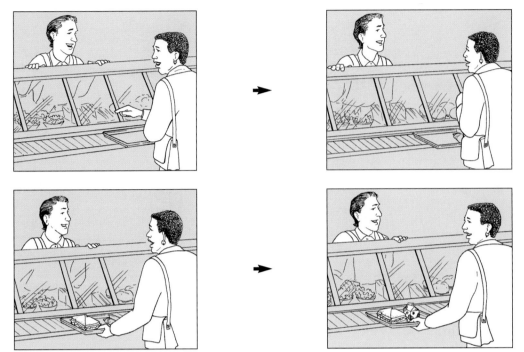

🎧 Listen again and repeat.

🎧 Listen and circle.

Pair work.

🎧 Look and listen.

P

🎧 Listen again and repeat.

🎧 Look and listen.

F

🎧 Listen again and repeat.

🎧 Listen and circle P or F.

1. Ⓟ F   2. P F   3. P F   4. P F   5. P F

6. P F   7. P F   8. P F   9. P F   10. P F

TEACHER

Literacy: Recognize sound-symbol correspondence of P and F as initial sound of known and unknown words.

🎧 **Listen and repeat.**

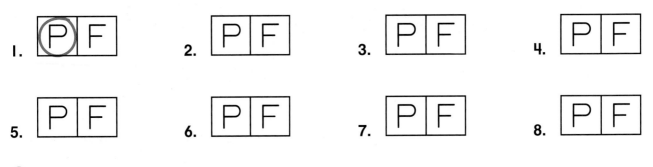

1. P F
2. P F
3. P F
4. P F

5. P F
6. P F
7. P F
8. P F

🎧 **Listen and circle P or F.**

Circle P and F.

P

PANTS   PASTA   PARKING LOT

F

FIVE   FIRE   FISH

TEACHER

Literacy: Discriminate between P and F as initial sound of known words.
Recognize letters P and F.
More practice: Worksheet 52 (Teacher's Edition CD-ROM).

🎧 Look and listen.

 →

🎧 Listen again and repeat.

Pair work.

TEACHER

Survival: Order food items by size. Recognize S, M, L as representing *small, medium, large.*
Civics concept: Restaurant food can often be ordered by size.
New language: Fries / small, medium, large (for foods).

🎧 **Look and listen.**

1. 2. 3.

🎧 **Listen again and repeat.**

🎧 **Look and listen.**

1. 2. 3. 4. 5.

6. 7. 8. 9.

🎧 **Listen again and repeat.**

🎧 **Listen and circle.**

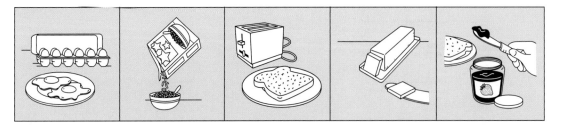

NAME _____

🎧 Look and listen.

V

🎧 Listen again and repeat.

🎧 Look and listen.

F 15

🎧 Listen again and repeat.

🎧 Listen and circle V or F.

1. (V) F   2. V F   3. V F   4. V F

5. V F   6. V F   7. V F   8. V F

Say the word. Circle V or F.

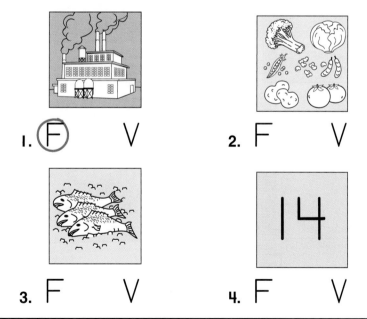

1. (F) V   2. F V

3. F V   4. F V

TEACHER

Literacy: Recognize sound-symbol correspondence of letter V.
  Discriminate between V and F as initial sound of known and unknown words.
More practice: Worksheet 53 (Teacher's Edition CD-ROM).

🎧 **Look and listen.**

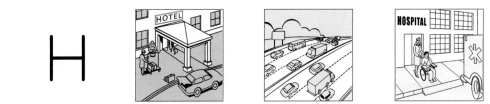

H

🎧 **Listen again and repeat.**

Say the word. Trace the letter.

H   H   H   H

Say the word. Circle the letter.

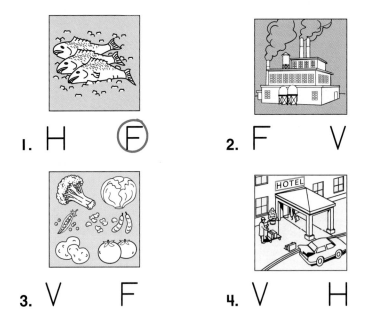

1. H   Ⓕ

2. F   V

3. V   F

4. V   H

TEACHER

Literacy: Recognize sound-symbol correspondence of letter H. Trace letter H. Discriminate between H, F, and V as initial sound of known words.
More practice: Worksheet 54 (Teacher's Edition CD-ROM).

🎧 **Look and listen.**

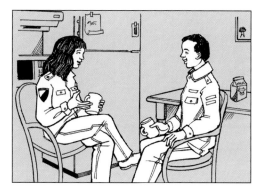

🎧 **Listen again and repeat.**

🎧 **Look and listen.**

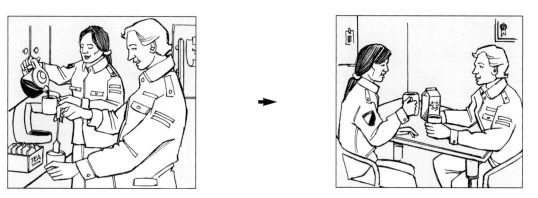

🎧 **Listen again and repeat.**

Pair work.

7:30   12:15   6:45

TEACHER

Survival: Exchange information about what one eats for various meals. Politely express likes and dislikes. Agree and disagree.

Civics concepts: It's expected that people's tastes vary. It's OK to compare tastes.

New language: What do you eat for [breakfast]? / I eat [eggs]. / I like [coffee]. / Not me. / Me too.

🎧 Listen and circle.

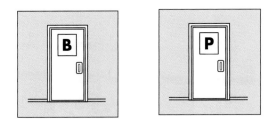

🎧 Look and listen.

🎧 Listen and respond.

I. **2.** **3.**

Trace.

M B F P V H

🎧 Listen and circle the letter.

1. [M | B]   2. [B | P]   3. [B | P]

4. [F | V]   5. [F | H]   6. [F | H]

Say the word. Trace the letter.

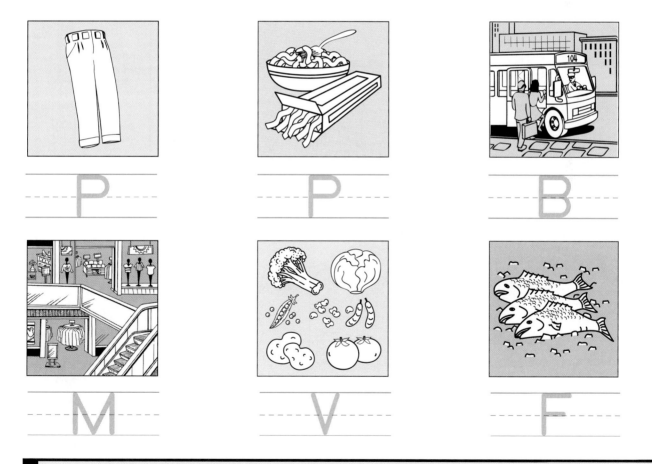

P   P   B

M   V   F

Talk about the picture. Role-play conversations.

TEACHER

Survival / civics review: Point and name things in the picture. Make sentences about the picture. Role-play conversations based on the picture.
Tests: Teacher's Edition CD-ROM.

114 • UNIT 6

🎧 **A. Look and listen.**

A ➤ B ➤ C ➤ D ➤ E ➤ F ➤ G

H ➤ I ➤ J ➤ K

L ➤ M ➤ N ➤ O ➤ P

Q ➤ R ➤ S

T ➤ U ➤ V

W ➤ X

Y ➤ Z

🎧 **B. Listen again and repeat.**

TEACHER

Literacy: Recognize that the alphabet has an order. Learn the the "names" of the letters in a rhythmic chant.

🎧 A. Listen and repeat.

A B C
X Y Z
E F G
N O P
R S T
T U V
C D E

🎧 B. Listen and repeat.

A J K
B C D   E G P   T V Z
F L M   N S X
A H
Q W
Y I

🎧 C. Listen and circle.

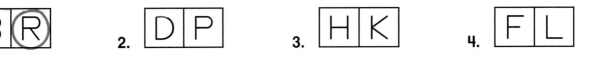

1. B ⓇR   2. D P   3. H K   4. F L

TEACHER

Literacy: Read, listen to, and repeat letters that have rhyming or otherwise related sound patterns.

🎧 **A. Look and listen.**

🎧 **B. Listen again and repeat.**

🎧 **C. Look and listen.**

🎧 **D. Listen again and repeat.**

🎧 **E. Listen and circle.**

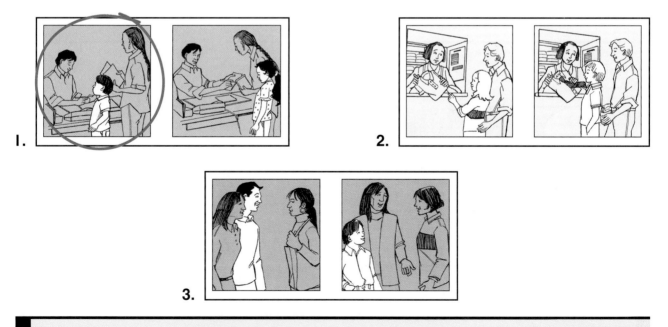

1.

2.

3.

TEACHER

Survival: Learn vocabulary for family and social relationships.
Civics concept: Wedding bands are commonly worn on the left hand.
New language: Father, mother, daughter, son, husband, wife, sister, brother, friend.

∩ A. Look and listen.

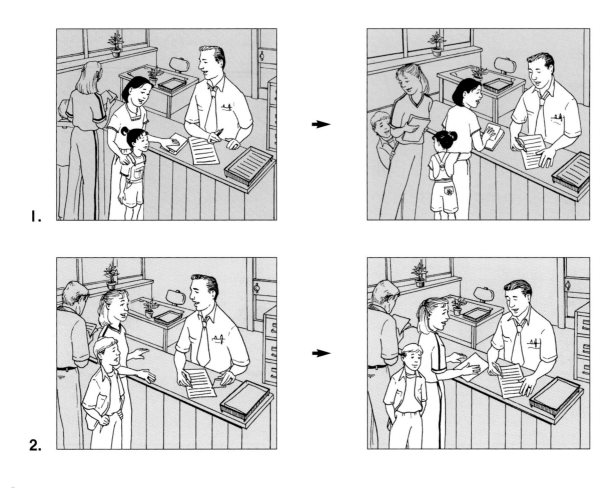

1.

2.

∩ B. Listen again and repeat.

C. Pair work.

A B C D E F G
H I J K L M N
O P Q R S T U
V W X Y Z

Survival: Ask for and spell names.
Civics concept: People often ask you to spell a name.
New language: This is my daughter [son]. / What's her [his] name? / How do you spell that?

A. Look at the capital and lowercase letters.

V v   W w   X x   Y y   Z z

B. Match.

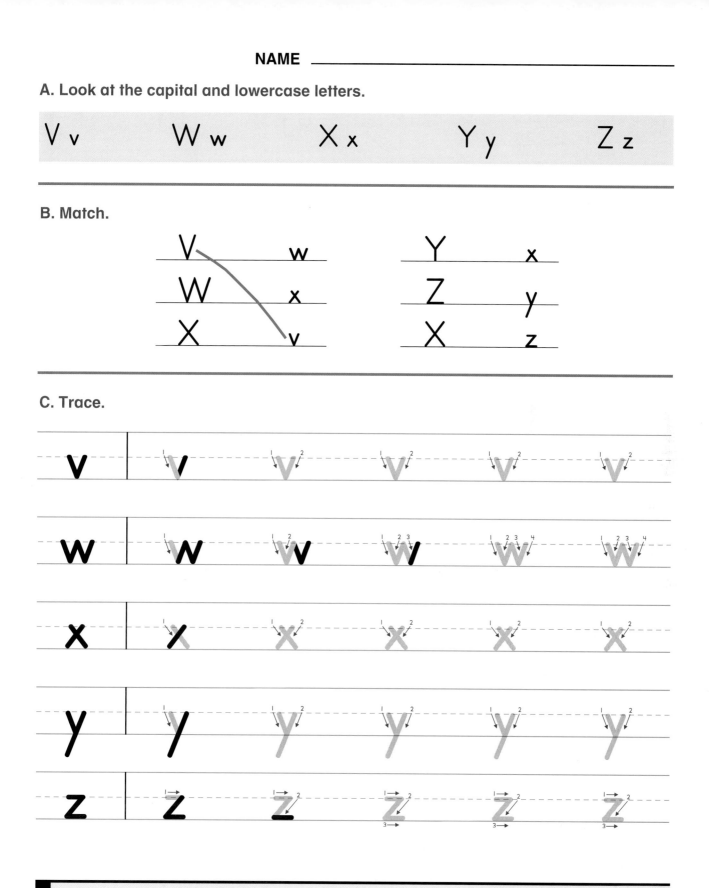

C. Trace.

TEACHER

Literacy: Recognize, read, and trace lowercase v, w, x, y, z. Match capital
   with lowercase letters.
More practice: Worksheets 56–57 (Teacher's Edition CD-ROM).

UNIT 7 • 119

A. Look at the capital and lowercase letters.

K k   L l   I i   J j   T t   F f

B. Circle.

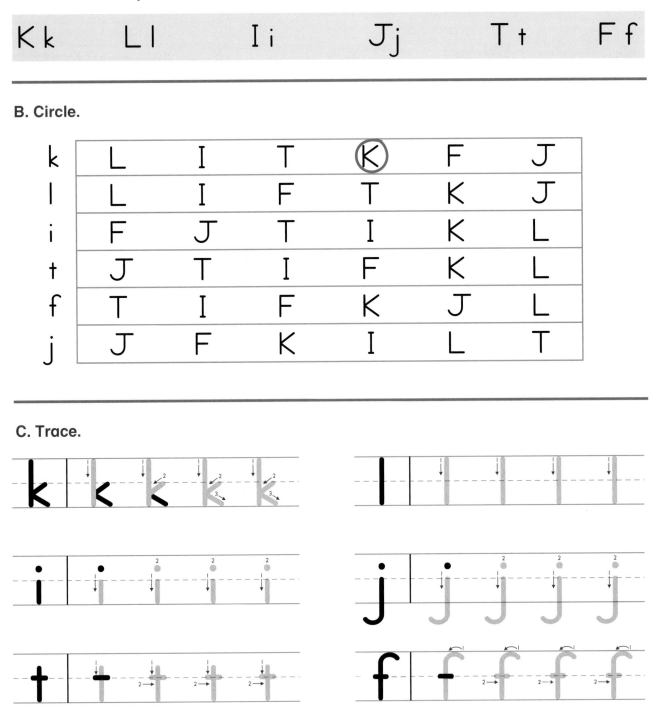

k	L	I	T	(K)	F	J
l	L	I	F	T	K	J
i	F	J	T	I	K	L
t	J	T	I	F	K	L
f	T	I	F	K	J	L
j	J	F	K	I	L	T

C. Trace.

k k k k k   l

i i i i   j j j j j

t t t t   f f f f f

Literacy: Recognize, read, and trace k, l, i, j, t, f. Match capital with lowercase letters.
More practice: Worksheets 58–59 (Teacher's Edition CD-ROM).

TEACHER

A. Look and listen.

2003

1993

1.

2.

B. Listen again and repeat.

C. Pair work.

10

4

A. Look and listen.

B. Listen again and repeat.

C. Pair work.

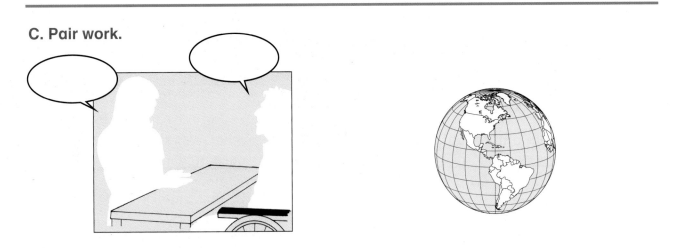

D. Look and listen.

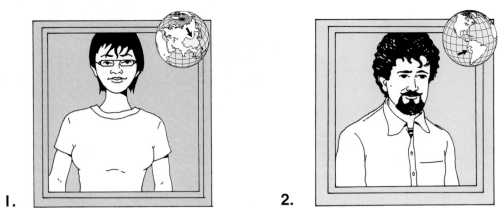

1.   2.

E. Listen again and repeat.

A. Look at the capital and lowercase letters.

R r   N n   M m   U u   H h

B. Circle.

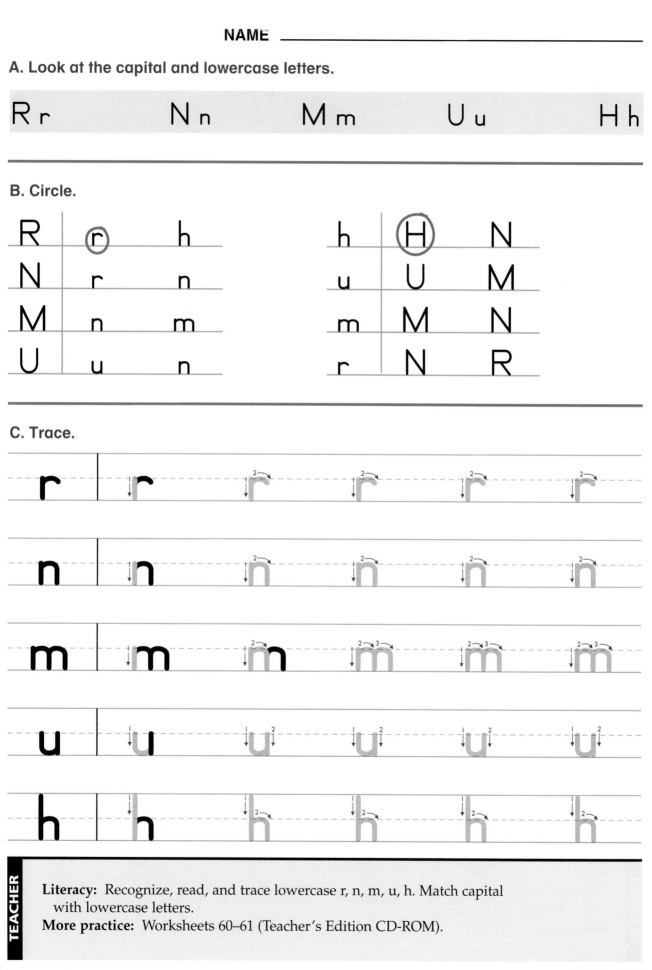

C. Trace.

A. Look at the capital and lowercase letters.

D d   P p   B b   A a   Q q   G g

B. Match.

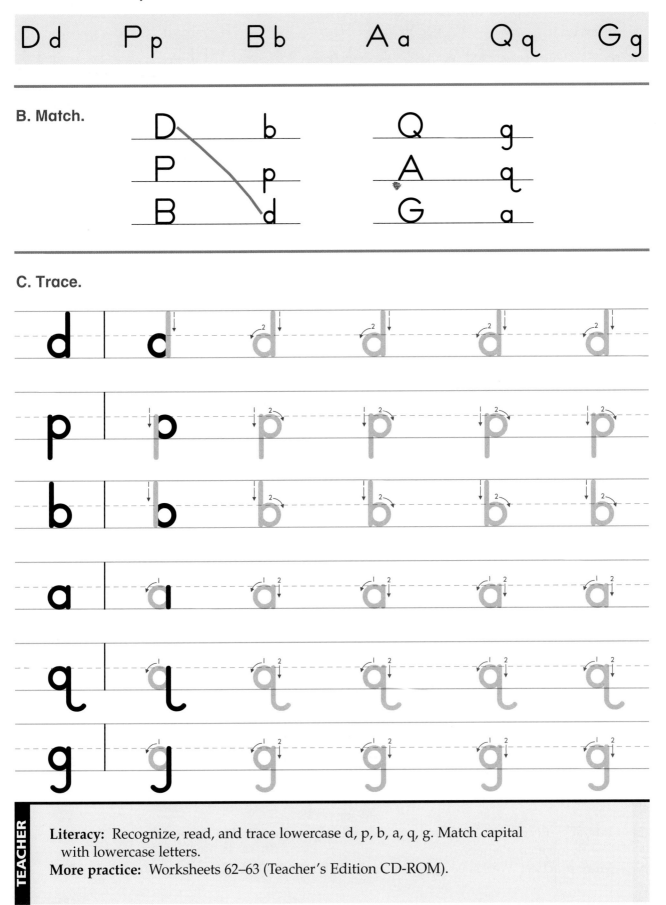

D		b
P		p
B		d

Q		g
A		q
G		a

C. Trace.

d   d   d   d   d   d

p   p   p   p   p   p

b   b   b   b   b   b

a   a   a   a   a   a

q   q   q   q   q   q

g   g   g   g   g   g

TEACHER

Literacy: Recognize, read, and trace lowercase d, p, b, a, q, g. Match capital with lowercase letters.

More practice: Worksheets 62–63 (Teacher's Edition CD-ROM).

∩ A. Look and listen.

1.   2.   3.   4.

5.

∩ B. Listen again and repeat.

∩ C. Listen and circle.

1.   2.

3.   4.

TEACHER

Survival: Learn vocabulary for marital status.
Civics concept: It's OK to ask questions about a person's marital status. Each status has a name.
New language: Single, married, separated, divorced, widowed.

⌒ A. Look and listen.

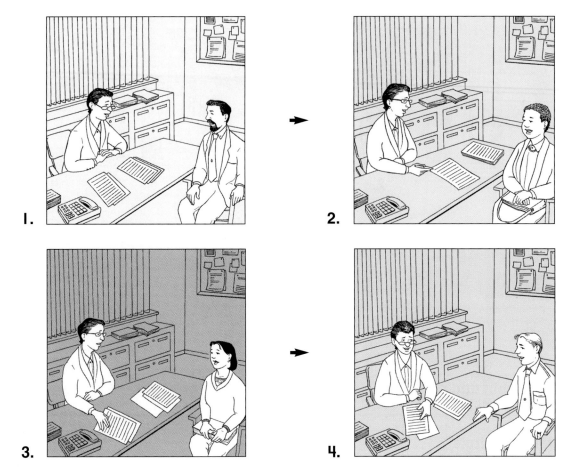

1.

2.

3.

4.

⌒ B. Listen again and repeat.

C. Pair work.

A. Look at the capital and lowercase letters.

O o   C c   E e   S s

B. Circle.

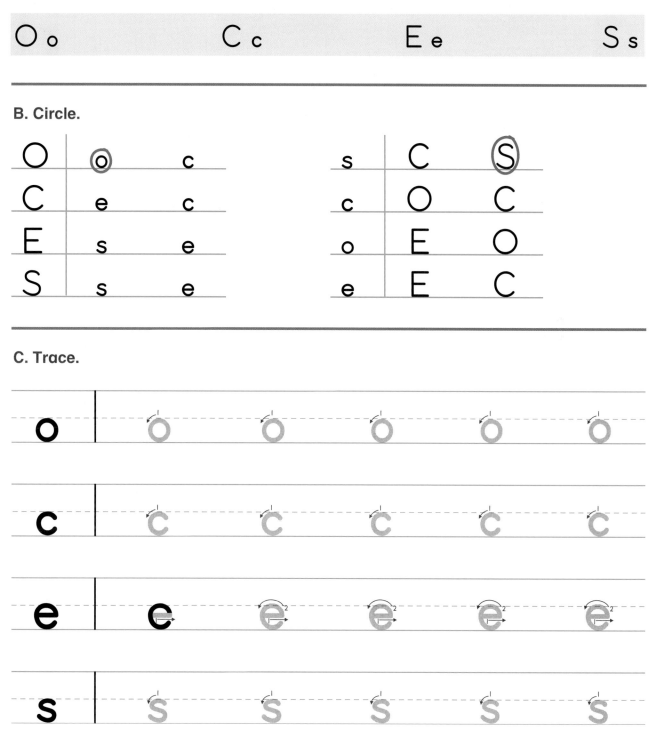

C. Trace.

o   o   o   o   o   o

c   c   c   c   c   c

e   e   e   e   e   e

s   s   s   s   s   s

TEACHER

Literacy: Recognize, read, and trace lowercase o, c, e, s. Match capital with lowercase letters.
More practice: Worksheets 64–65 (Teacher's Edition CD-ROM).

A. Look.

Tim   Baker

first name   last name

B. Write <u>your</u> name.

first name   last name

first name   last name

TEACHER

Literacy: Write your own name on a form, using capital and lowercase letters.
Sight words: First name, last name.
More practice: Worksheet 66 (Teacher's Edition CD-ROM).

A. Look and listen.

B. Listen again and repeat.

C. Listen and circle.

1.

2.

D. Look and listen.

E. Listen again and repeat.

A. Listen. Circle the name.

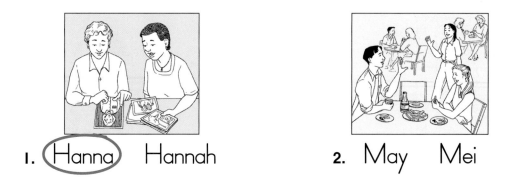

1. (Hanna)   Hannah

2. May   Mei

B. Look and listen.

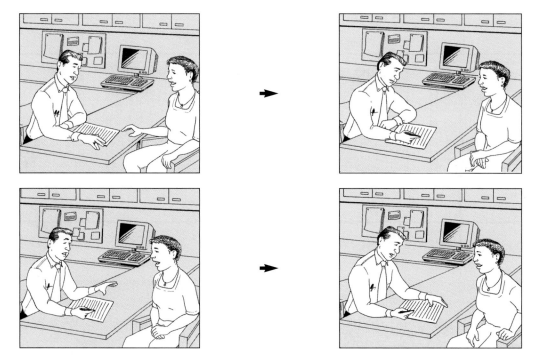

C. Listen and respond.

1.   2.   3.

Circle.

a	(A)	D	b	P	B
c	C	E	d	D	B
e	O	E	f	T	F
g	G	Q	h	N	H
i	J	I	j	J	F
k	H	K	l	I	L
m	M	W	n	U	N
o	O	D	p	D	P
q	P	Q	r	R	B
s	Z	S	t	J	T
u	A	U	v	Y	V
w	V	W	x	Z	X
y	X	Y	z	Z	L

TEACHER

Literacy review: Review correspondence of capital and lowercase letters in alphabetical order.

More practice: Worksheet 67 (Teacher's Edition CD-ROM).

Literacy test: Teacher's Edition CD-ROM.

Talk about the pictures. Role-play conversations.

TEACHER

Survival / civics review: Point and name things in the pictures. Make sentences about the pictures. Role-play conversations based on the pictures.
Tests: Teacher's Edition CD-ROM.

🎧 **A. Look and listen.**

D d

S	M	T	W	T	F	S
		1	2	3	4	5	6
7	8	9	10	11	12	13
14	15	16	17	18	19	20
21	22	23	24	25	26	27
28	29	30	31			

🎧 **B. Listen again and repeat.**

🎧 **C. Look and listen.**

Z z

33616

🎧 **D. Listen again and repeat.**

🎧 **E. Listen and circle.**

1. D Z
2. D Z
3. D Z
4. D Z

5. D Z
6. D Z
7. D Z
8. D Z

F. Trace.

S	M	T	W	T	F	S
		1	2	3	4	5	6
7	8	9	10	11	12	13
14	15	16	17	18	19	20
21	22	23	24	25	26	27
28	29	30	31			

DAY DINNER ZIP CODE

TEACHER

Literacy: Recognize sound-symbol correspondence of D and Z as initial sound of known and unknown words. Trace D and Z.

A. Say the word. Circle D or Z.

1. (D)   Z

2. D   Z

3. D   Z

4. D   Z

5. D   Z

6. D   Z

🎧 B. Listen and trace.

DAY   ZIP CODE   DRESS

TEACHER

Literacy: Discriminate between D and Z as initial sound of known words.
Listen and trace D and Z.
More practice: Worksheet 68 (Teacher's Edition CD-ROM).

A. Look and listen.

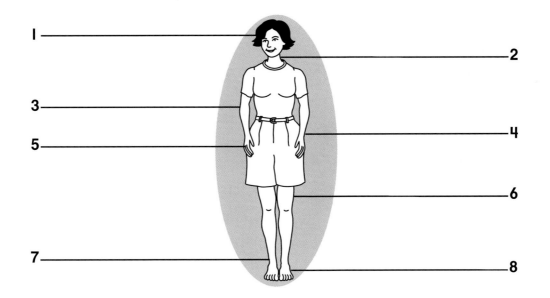

1	2
3	4
5	6
7	8

B. Listen again and repeat.

C. Listen and write.

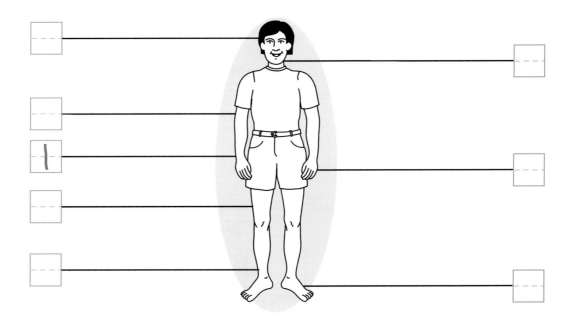

Survival: Learn vocabulary for names of body parts.
New language: Head, neck, arm, wrist, hand, leg, ankle, foot.

A. Look and listen.

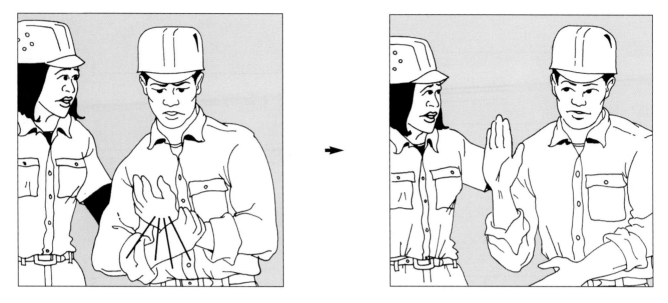

B. Listen again and repeat.

C. Pair work.

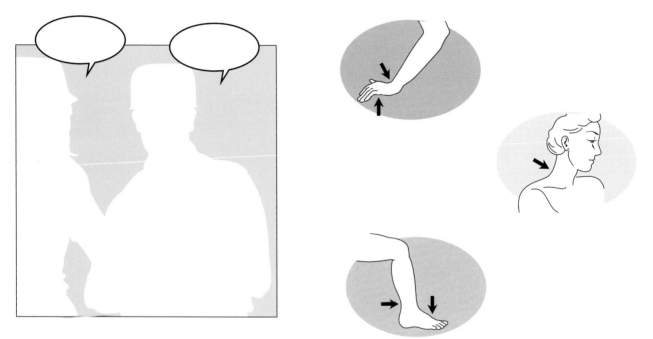

TEACHER

Survival: Report an injury, express concern, offer to get help, decline help.
Civics concept: You're expected to offer help to someone who is hurt or injured.
New language: What's wrong? / I hurt my [hand]. / Should I get help? / No, thanks. / I'm OK.

🎧 **A. Look and listen.**

S s

🎧 **B. Listen again and repeat.**

🎧 **C. Look and listen.**

T t 10

🎧 **D. Listen again and repeat.**

🎧 **E. Listen and circle.**

1. S (T)

2. S T

3. S T

4. S T

5. S T

6. S T

7. S T

8. S T

F. Trace.

6

SIX

SON

TAXI

TEACHER

Literacy: Recognize sound-symbol correspondence of S and T. Discriminate between S and T as initial sound of known and unknown words. Trace S and T.

A. Say the word. Circle the letter.

1. (S)   T

2. S   T

3. S   T

4. S   T

5. D   Z

6. S   Z

May Banks
2 B Street
Bay City, FL 33605

🎧 **B. Listen and trace.**

SON   SIX   TEN

TEACHER

Literacy: Discriminate between S, T, D, and Z as initial sound of known words. Trace S and T.
More practice: Worksheet 69 (Teacher's Edition CD-ROM).

🎧 A. Look and listen.

1.

2.

3.

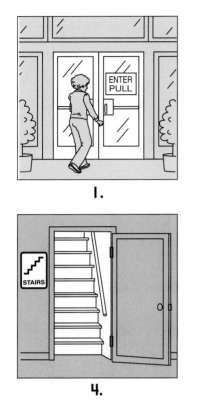

4.

5.

6.

🎧 B. Listen again and repeat.

C. Match.

1. ENTER

2. STAIRS

3. RESTROOMS

A. Look and listen. 🎧

1.   2.   3.   4.   5.

B. Listen again and repeat. 🎧

C. Look and listen. 🎧

1.   2.

D. Listen again and repeat. 🎧

E. Pair work.

🎧 **A. Look and listen.**

N n

		NOVEMBER			
1	2	3	4	5	6
7	8	9	10	11	12	13
14	15	16	17	18	19	20
21	22	23	24	25	26	27
28	29	30			

🎧 **B. Listen again and repeat.**

🎧 **C. Look and listen.**

J j

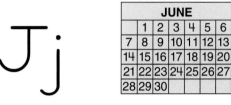

		JUNE			
1	2	3	4	5	6
7	8	9	10	11	12	13
14	15	16	17	18	19	20
21	22	23	24	25	26	27
28	29	30			

🎧 **D. Listen again and repeat.**

🎧 **E. Listen and circle.**

1. Ⓝ J   2. N J   3. N J   4. N J

5. N J   6. N J   7. N J   8. N J

F. Trace.

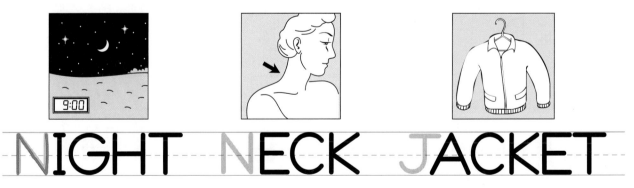

NIGHT   NECK   JACKET

TEACHER

Literacy: Recognize sound-symbol correspondence of N and J. Discriminate between N and J as initial sound of known and unknown words. Trace N and J.

A. Say the word. Circle the letter.

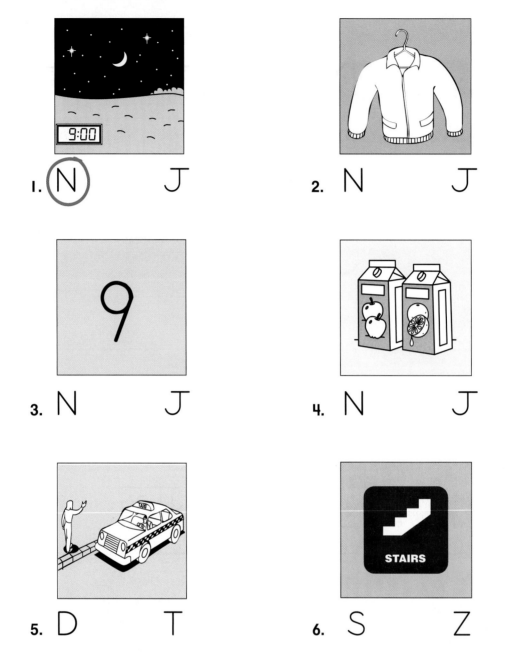

1. Ⓝ   J

2. N   J

3. N   J

4. N   J

5. D   T

6. S   Z

🎧 **B. Listen and trace.**

JUNE   NAME   JULY

TEACHER

Literacy: Discriminate between N, J, D, T, S, and Z as initial sound of known words. Trace N and J.
More practice: Worksheet 70 (Teacher's Edition CD-ROM).

⌒ A. Look and listen.

1.   2.   3.

⌒ B. Listen again and repeat.

C. Match.

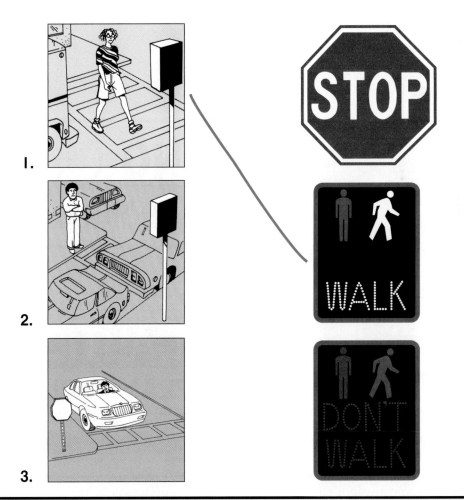

1.

2.

3.

Survival: Recognize and demonstrate understanding of common street signs.
Civics concept: Signs protect your safety and that of others. Obey them.
Sight words: STOP, WALK, DON'T WALK.

TEACHER

🎧 **A. Look and listen.**

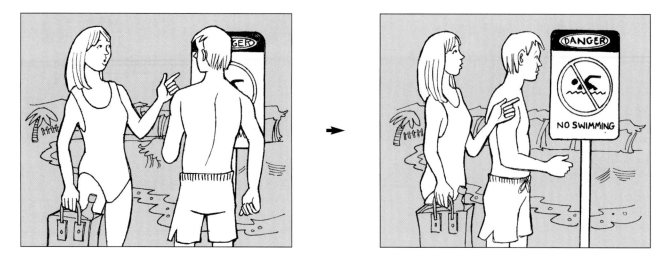

🎧 **B. Listen again and repeat.**

🎧 **C. Look and listen.**

1.

2.

3.

4.

🎧 **D. Listen again and repeat.**

A. Circle.

M	m	w
B	p	b
P	d	p
F	f	t
D	d	a

T	j	t
S	z	s
N	u	n
J	j	f

B. Trace.

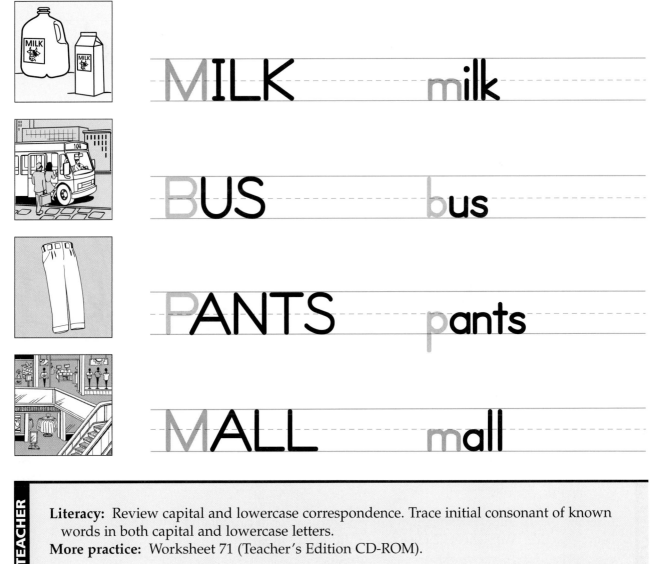

MILK   milk

BUS   bus

PANTS   pants

MALL   mall

TEACHER

Literacy: Review capital and lowercase correspondence. Trace initial consonant of known words in both capital and lowercase letters.
More practice: Worksheet 71 (Teacher's Edition CD-ROM).

Trace.

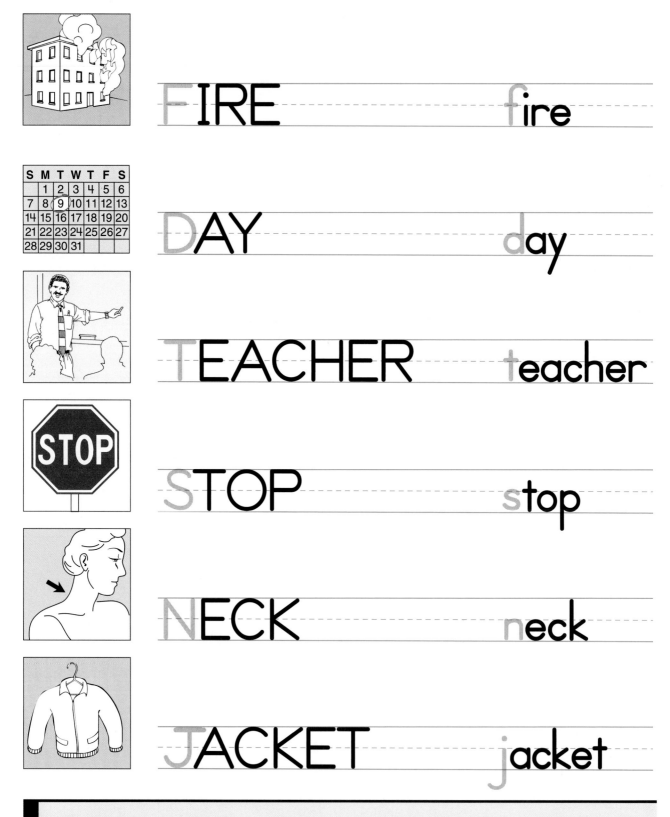

FIRE   fire

DAY   day

TEACHER   teacher

STOP   stop

NECK   neck

JACKET   jacket

🎧 A. Look and listen.

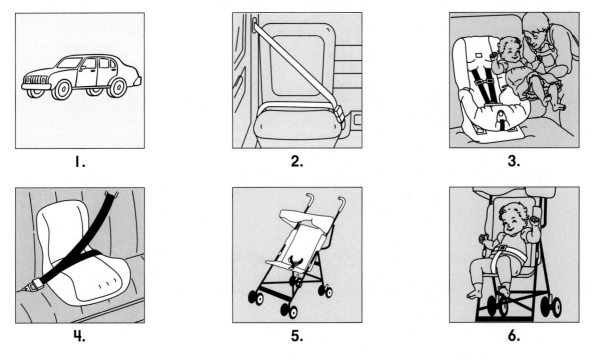

1.

2.

3.

4.

5.

6.

🎧 B. Listen again and repeat.

🎧 C. Look and listen.

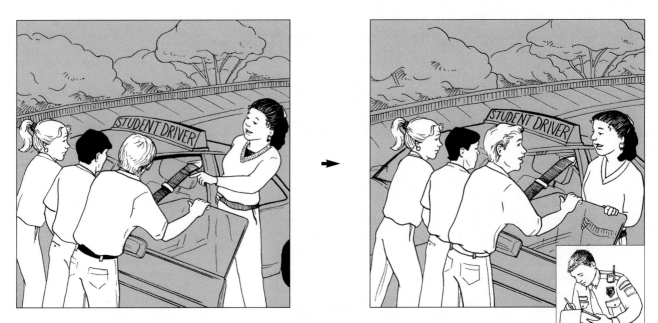

🎧 D. Listen again and repeat.

TEACHER

Survival: Learn vocabulary for passenger restraints. Understand necessity of using passenger restraints in vehicles.

Civics concept: The law requires safety restraints. You must obey the law.

New language: Car, seat belt, car seat, booster seat, stroller, safety harness / You have to use a [seat belt]. / Why? / It's the law.

🎧 **A. Listen and circle.**

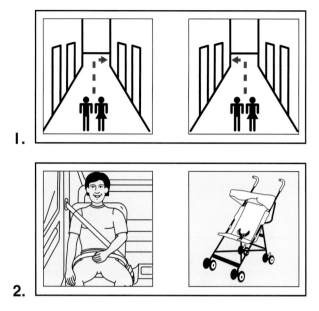

I.

2.

🎧 **B. Look and listen.**

🎧 **C. Listen and respond.**

I.   2.   3.

TEACHER

Authentic practice: Students listen to an authentic conversation at a medical reception desk and then complete listening and speaking tasks, providing true information about themselves.

NAME _____

A. Circle.

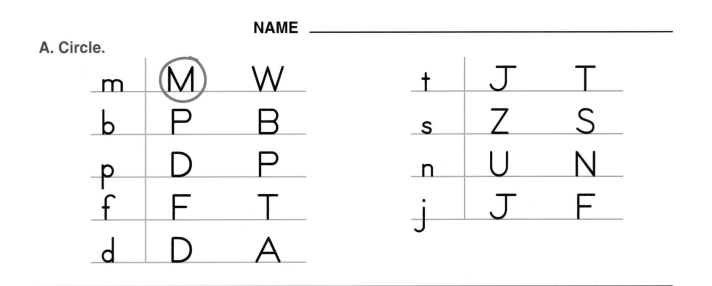

m	(M)	W
b	P	B
p	D	P
f	F	T
d	D	A

t	J	T
s	Z	S
n	U	N
j	J	F

B. Trace.

STOP   stop

MALL   mall

BANK   bank

FIRE   fire

DANGER   danger

Talk about the picture. Role-play conversations.

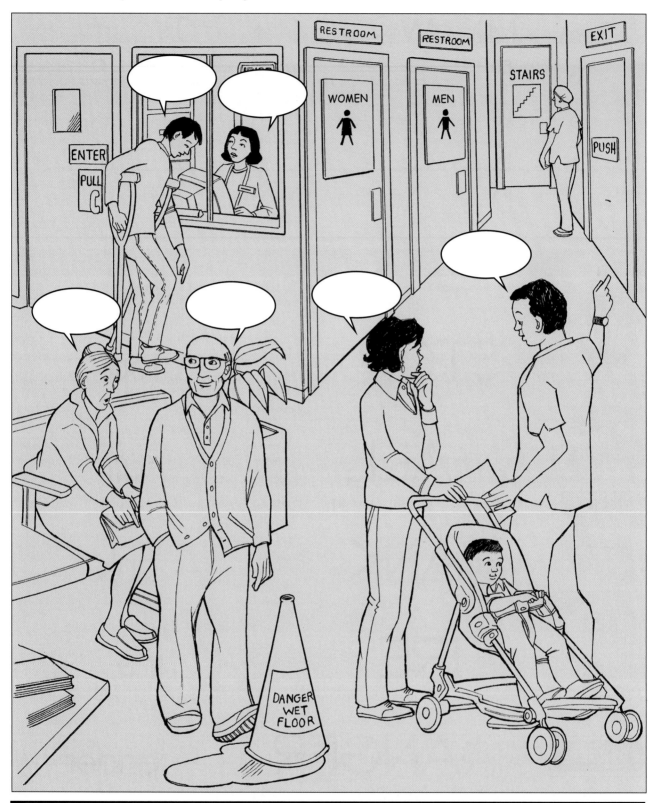

TEACHER

Survival / civics review: Point and name things in the picture. Make sentences about the picture. Role-play conversations based on the picture.
Tests: Teacher's Edition CD-ROM.

150 • UNIT 8

🎧 A. Look and listen.

C c   CAUTION

🎧 B. Listen again and repeat.

🎧 C. Look and listen.

G g

🎧 D. Listen again and repeat.

🎧 E. Listen and circle.

1. Ⓒ G   2. C G   3. C G   4. C G

5. C G   6. C G   7. C G   8. C G

F. Trace and write.

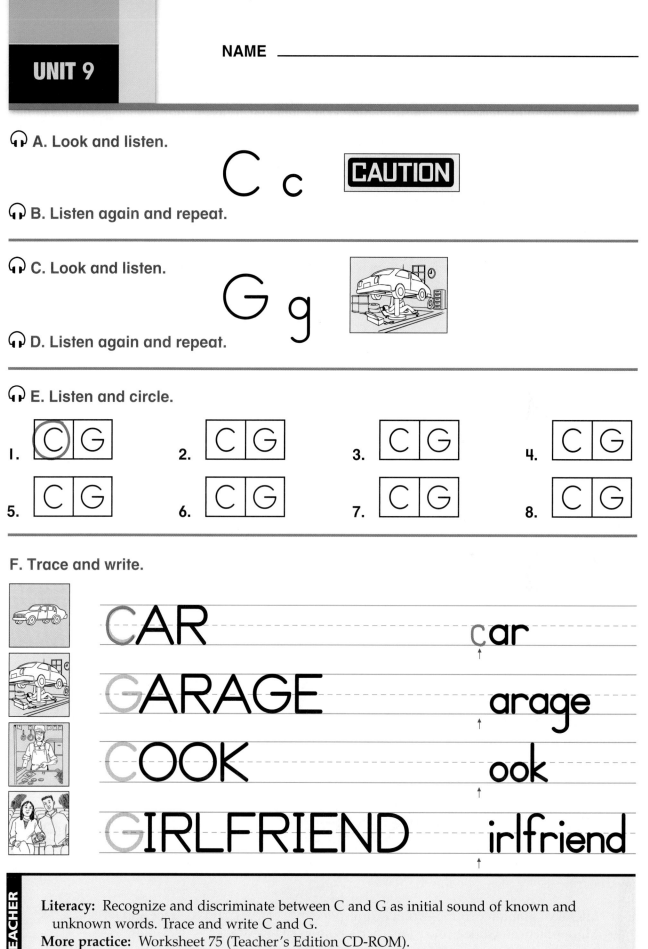

CAR _____ car

GARAGE _____ arage

COOK _____ ook

GIRLFRIEND _____ irlfriend

TEACHER

Literacy: Recognize and discriminate between C and G as initial sound of known and unknown words. Trace and write C and G.
More practice: Worksheet 75 (Teacher's Edition CD-ROM).

🎧 **A. Look and listen.**

K k
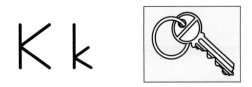

🎧 **B. Listen again and repeat.**

🎧 **C. Listen and circle.**

1. (k) l g   2. k l g   3. k l g   4. k l g

D. Trace and write.

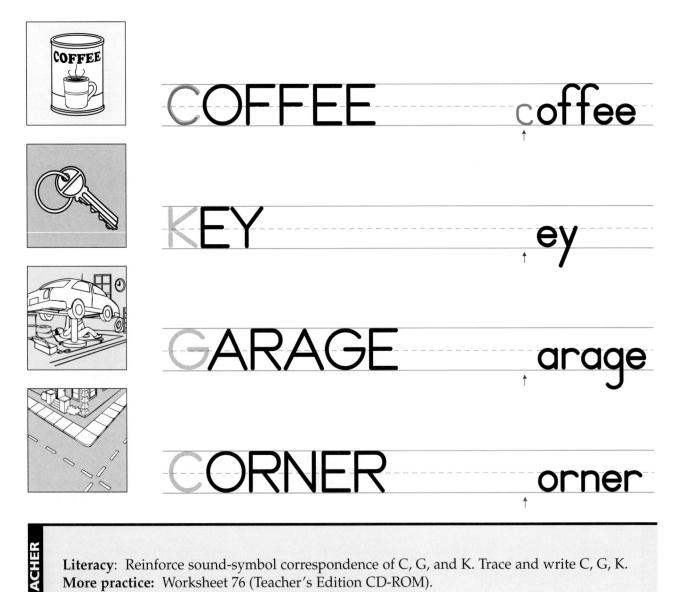

COFFEE   coffee

KEY   ey

GARAGE   arage

CORNER   orner

TEACHER

Literacy: Reinforce sound-symbol correspondence of C, G, and K. Trace and write C, G, K.
More practice: Worksheet 76 (Teacher's Edition CD-ROM).

🎧 A. Look and listen.

1. $1.00

2. $5.00

3. $10.00

4. $20.00

5. $50.00

6. $100.00

🎧 B. Listen again and repeat.

🎧 C. Look and listen.

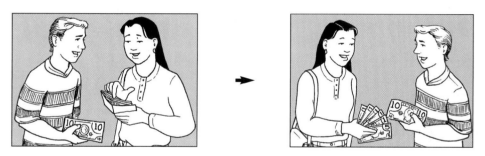

🎧 D. Listen again and repeat.

E. Pair work.

TEACHER

Survival: Recognize U.S. bills and understand their monetary value. Ask for change.
Civics concept: It's OK to ask a stranger for change.
New language: A dollar, five, ten, twenty, fifty, a hundred dollars / Do you have change for [$10]? / Let me check. / Here you go. / Thanks so much.

A. Look and listen.

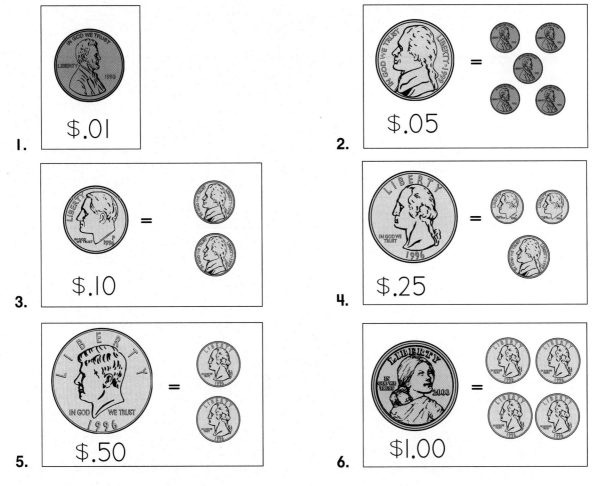

1. $.01

2. $.05

3. $.10

4. $.25

5. $.50

6. $1.00

B. Listen again and repeat.

C. Match.

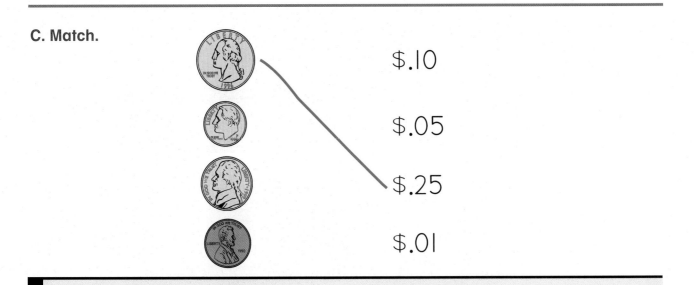

$.10

$.05

$.25

$.01

TEACHER

Survival: Recognize U.S. coins and understand their monetary value.
Civics concept: Money comes in the form of coins as well as bills.
New language: Penny, nickel, dime, quarter, half dollar.

NAME _____

🎧 A. Look and listen.

1. $5.50   2. $3.75   3. $22.25   4. $14.63   5. $12.08

🎧 B. Listen again and repeat.

C. Look and trace.

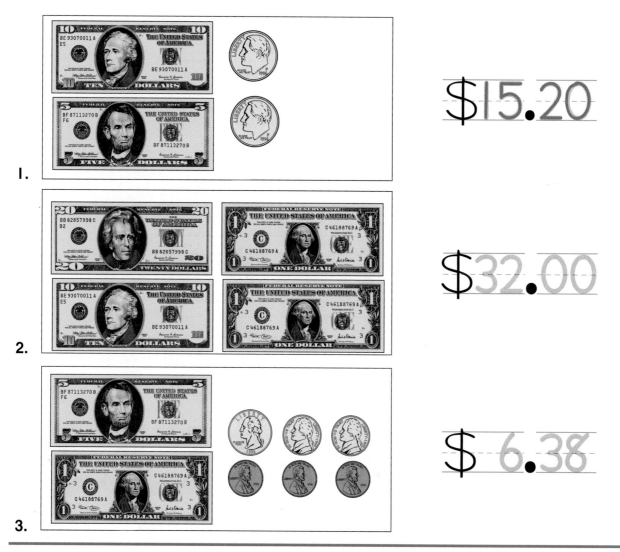

1. $15.20

2. $32.00

3. $ 6.38

D. Read the amounts. Say the amounts.

$7.34 $26.88 $49.12 $11.69

🎧 **A. Listen and circle.**

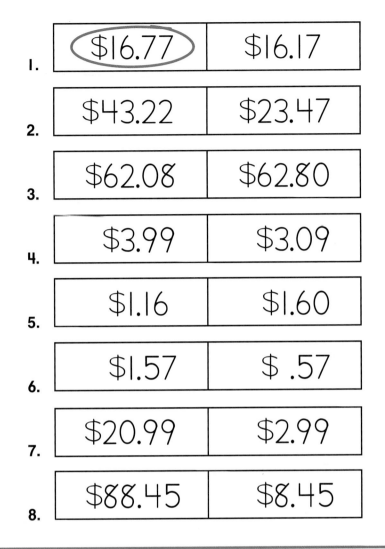

1.	$16.77	$16.17
2.	$43.22	$23.47
3.	$62.08	$62.80
4.	$3.99	$3.09
5.	$1.16	$1.60
6.	$1.57	$ .57
7.	$20.99	$2.99
8.	$88.45	$8.45

🎧 **B. Listen and write.**

1. $5.50

2. $35.6

3. $26.5

4. $9.

5. $ 1.

6. $ .00

A. Look and listen.

B. Listen again and repeat.

C. Pair work.

TEACHER

Survival: Order and pay for food. Choose item and size from a menu.
Civics concept: Menus tell you the cost of food items.
New language: That's [$2.78].

A. Look and listen.

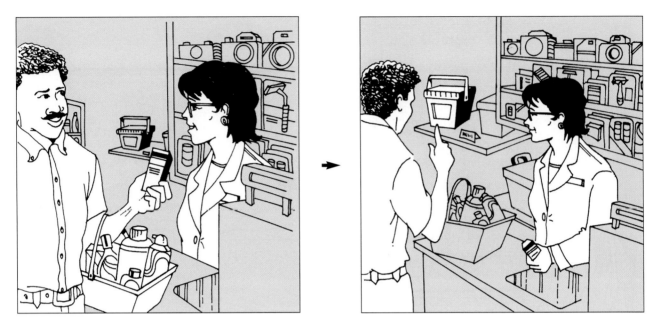

B. Listen again and repeat.

C. Pair work.

$1.99 + tax $2.24 + tax

$6.89 + tax $22.00 + tax

$2.99 + tax $10.50 + tax

TEACHER

Survival: Ask for prices of near and far singular items.
Civics concepts: It's OK to ask salespeople for a price. A sales tax is charged on many items.
New language: How much is this [that]? / plus tax.

🎧 **A. Look and listen.**

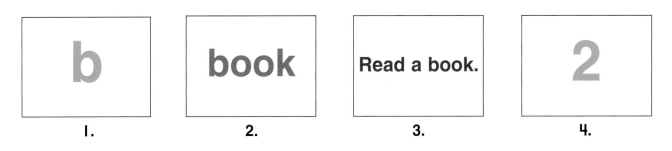

b	book	Read a book.	2
1.	2.	3.	4.

🎧 **B. Listen again and repeat.**

🎧 **C. Look at the picture. Circle the words.**

🎧 **D. Look at the picture. Circle the numbers.**

🎧 **E. Look at the picture. Circle the sentence.**

TEACHER

Literacy: Recognize symbols as numbers, letters, words, or sentences.

A. Cross out.

6	7	3	~~EXIT~~
14	STOP	8	56
A	R	J	8
m	3	b	s
PUSH	PULL	ENTER	f

B. Circle the words.

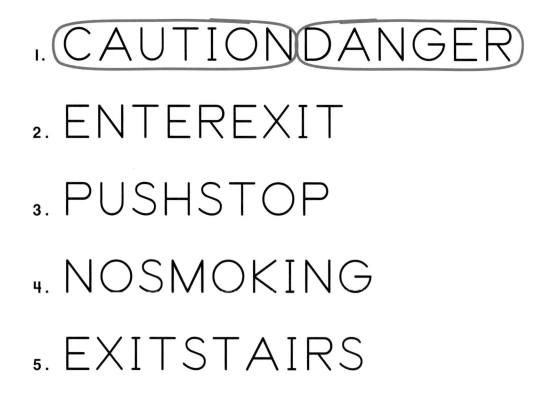

1. (CAUTION)(DANGER)

2. ENTEREXIT

3. PUSHSTOP

4. NOSMOKING

5. EXITSTAIRS

A. Look and listen.

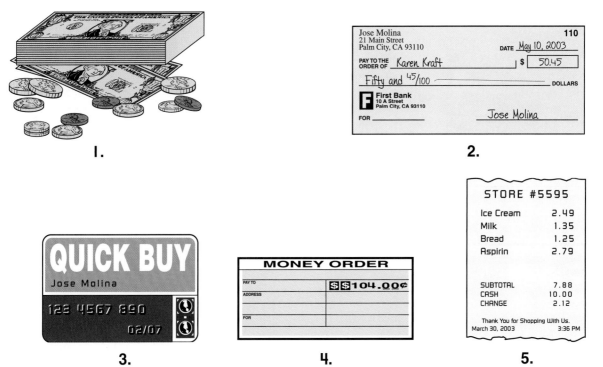

1.

Jose Molina
21 Main Street
Palm City, CA 93110

110

DATE May 10, 2003

PAY TO THE ORDER OF Karen Kraft $ 50.45

Fifty and 45/100 ———————————— DOLLARS

F First Bank
10 A Street
Palm City, CA 93110

FOR _____   Jose Molina

2.

QUICK BUY
Jose Molina
123 4567 890
02/07

3.

MONEY ORDER
PAY TO $$104.00¢
ADDRESS
FOR

4.

STORE #5595

Ice Cream   2.49
Milk   1.35
Bread   1.25
Aspirin   2.79

SUBTOTAL   7.88
CASH   10.00
CHANGE   2.12

Thank You for Shopping With Us.
March 30, 2003   3:36 PM

5.

B. Listen again and repeat.

C. Listen and circle.

1.

STORE #5595

Milk   1.35
Bread   1.25

SUBTOTAL   2.60
CASH   10.00
CHANGE   7.40

2.

QUICK BUY
Jose Molina
123 4567 890
02/07

3.

MONEY ORDER
PAY TO $$104.00¢
ADDRESS
FOR

A. Look and listen.

1.   2.   3.

B. Listen again and repeat.

C. Pair work.

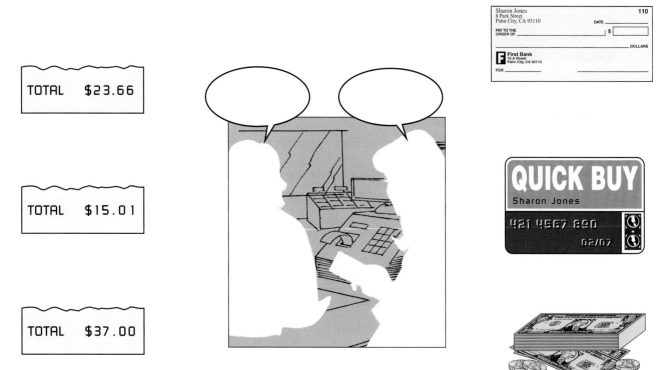

| TOTAL | $23.66 |

| TOTAL | $15.01 |

| TOTAL | $37.00 |

Sharon Jones
8 Park Street
Palm City, CA 93110

110

DATE _____

PAY TO THE
ORDER OF _____ | $ _____

_____ DOLLARS

First Bank
10 A Street
Palm City, CA 93110

FOR _____   _____

QUICK BUY
Sharon Jones
421 4567 890
02/07

TEACHER

Survival: Ask and answer questions about payment.

Civics concept: Payment can be made with a variety of devices other than cash.
It's OK to ask for a receipt.

New language: Will that be cash or charge? / Cash. / Charge. / Can I have a receipt?

Circle.

1. $10.00	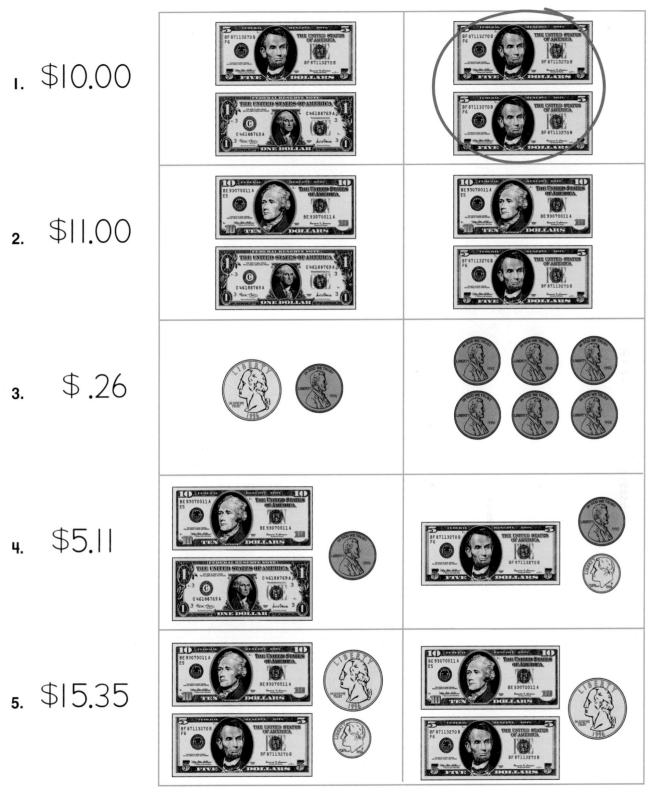	
2. $11.00		
3. $ .26		
4. $5.11		
5. $15.35		

TEACHER

Literacy: Recognize correct combinations of bills and coins to achieve a specified amount.
More practice: Worksheet 80 (Teacher's Edition CD-ROM).

🎧 A. Look and listen.

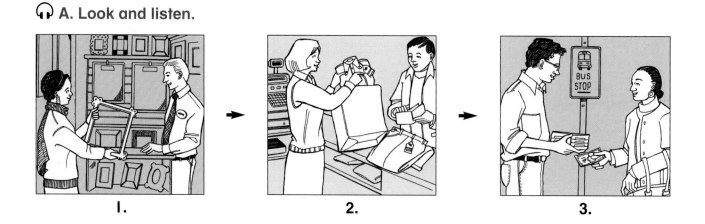

1.   2.   3.

🎧 B. Listen and circle.

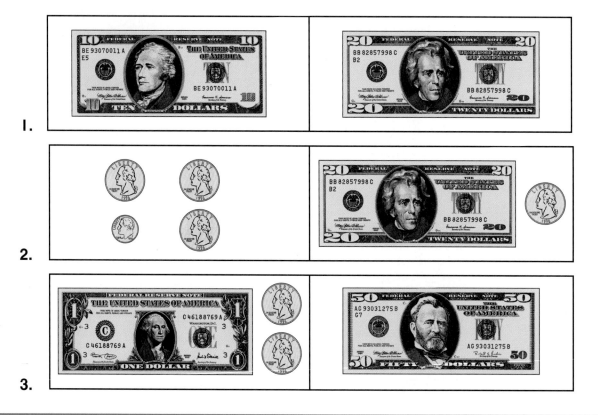

1.

2.

3.

🎧 C. Listen and trace.

$10.00 $20.25 $1.50

TEACHER

Literacy: Understand, circle, and trace spoken monetary amounts.
More practice: Worksheet 81 (Teacher's Edition CD-ROM).

⌒ A. Look and listen.

⌒ B. Listen again and repeat.

C. Pair work.

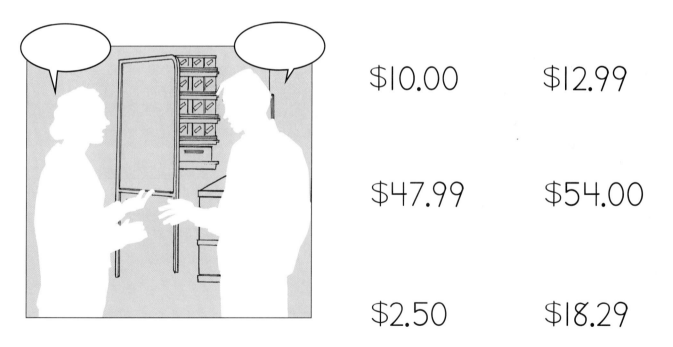

$10.00 $12.99

$47.99 $54.00

$2.50 $18.29

🎧 A. Listen and circle.

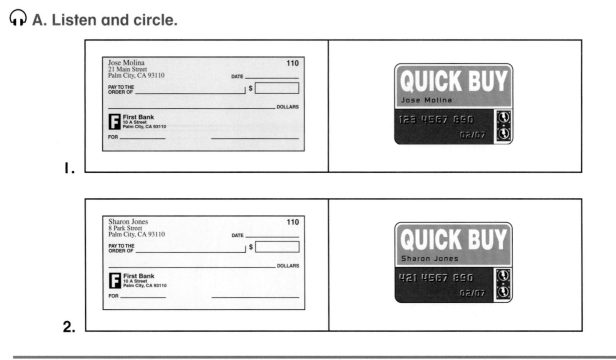

1.

2.

🎧 B. Look and listen.

🎧 C. Listen and respond.

1.

2.

3.

🎧 **A. Listen and circle.**

1. (m) b   2. p | f   3. v | h   4. d | t

5. s | z   6. n | j   7. g | p   8. m | b

B. Write.

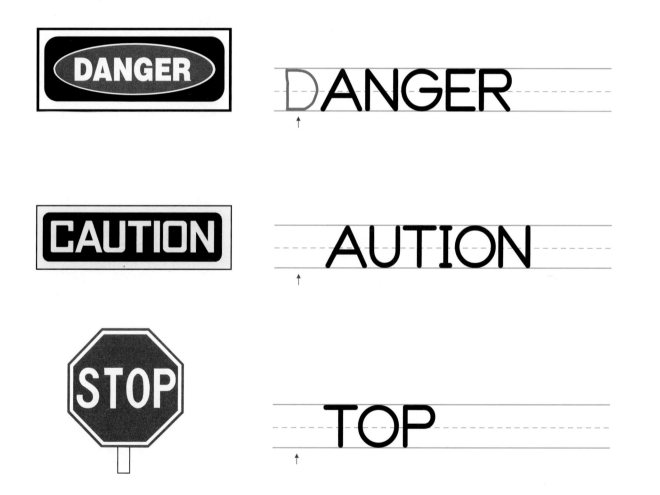

DANGER

AUTION

TOP

TEACHER

Literacy review: Write initial consonants in known words. Demonstrate recognition of sight words as groups of letters.

More practice: Worksheet 82 (Teacher's Edition CD-ROM).

Literacy test: Teacher's Edition CD-ROM.

Talk about the pictures. Role-play conversations.

TEACHER

Survival / civics review: Point and name things in the pictures. Make statements about the pictures. Role-play conversations based on the pictures.
Tests: Teacher's Edition CD-ROM.

168 • UNIT 9

🎧 **A. Look and listen.**

L l

🎧 **B. Listen again and repeat.**

🎧 **C. Look and listen.**

Y y

🎧 **D. Listen again and repeat.**

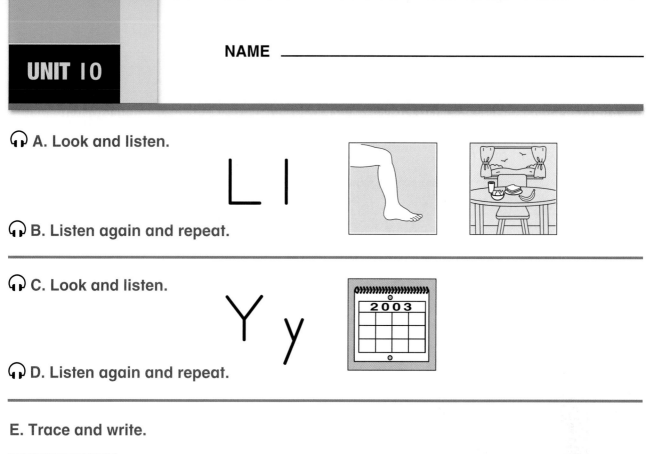

E. Trace and write.

LARGE   large

LATE   ate

YEAR   ear

A. Look and listen.

R r

B. Listen again and repeat.

C. Look and listen.

W w

D. Listen again and repeat.

E. Trace and write.

RESTROOM   restroom

RICE   ice

WALK   alk

WATER   ater

TEACHER

Literacy: Recognize sound-symbol correspondence of R and W. Trace and write initial capital and lowercase R and W for known words.

More practice: Worksheet 83 (Teacher's Edition CD-ROM).

A. Look and listen.

1.
2.
3.
4.
5.
6.

My name is Elena Silva.

7.
8.
9.

B. Listen again and repeat.

C. Listen and match.

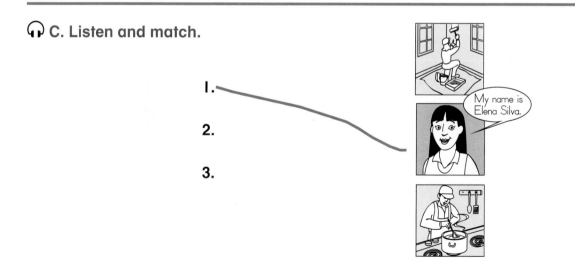

1.
2.
3.

My name is Elena Silva.

A. Look and listen.

B. Listen again and repeat.

C. Pair work.

NAME _____

🎧 **A. Look and listen.**

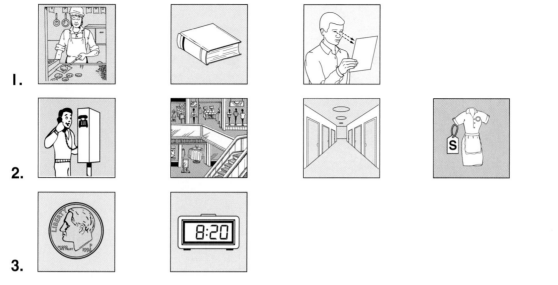

1.

2.

3.

🎧 **B. Listen again and repeat.**

🎧 **C. Look and listen.**

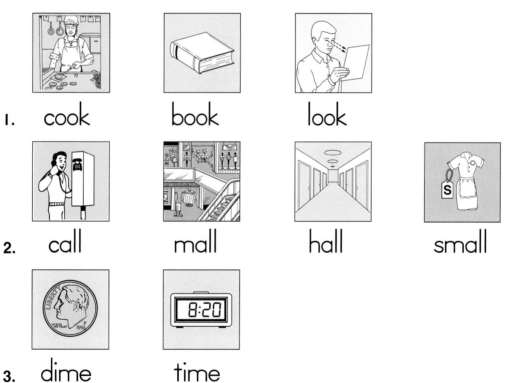

1.   cook   book   look

2.   call   mall   hall   small

3.   dime   time

🎧 **D. Listen again and repeat.**

TEACHER

Literacy: Recognize rhyming words and associate them with printed words.
More practice: Worksheet 84 (Teacher's Edition CD-ROM).

🎧 **A. Look and listen.**

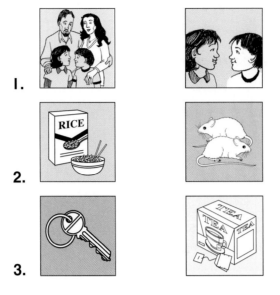

1.

2.

3.

🎧 **B. Listen again and repeat.**

🎧 **C. Look and listen.**

1. mother   brother

2. rice   mice

3. key   tea

🎧 **D. Listen again and repeat.**

TEACHER

Literacy: Recognize rhyming words and associate them with printed words.
More practice: Worksheet 85 (Teacher's Edition CD-ROM).

A. Look and listen.

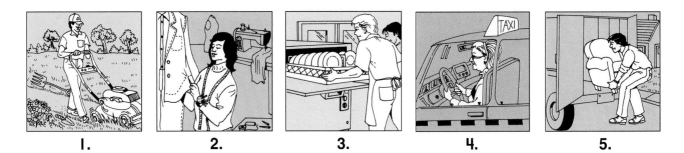

1.   2.   3.   4.   5.

B. Listen again and repeat.

C. Look and listen.

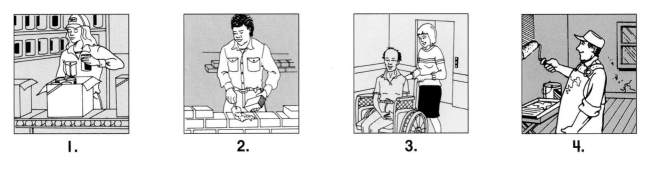

1.   2.   3.   4.

D. Listen again and repeat.

E. Listen and circle.

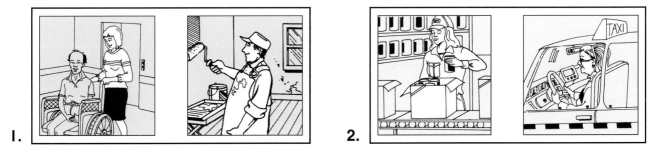

1.   2.

TEACHER

Survival: Learn vocabulary for occupations that don't require reading and writing or high-level proficiency in English.

Civics concept: Adults of all ages, races, and both sexes can do many jobs.

New language: Gardener, tailor, dishwasher, taxi driver, mover, packer, mason, companion, painter.

A. Look, listen, and read.

B. Listen again and repeat.

C. Look and listen.

D. Listen again and repeat.

E. Pair work.

TEACHER

Survival: Describe work experience in the U.S.

Civics concepts: Potential employers ask about prior work experience. It's important to give correct information.

New language: Do you have any experience in this country? / Yes, I do. / No, I don't. / right now / unemployed.

NAME _____

A. Cross out.

1.	Yes, I do.	~~Yes, Ido.~~
2.	No, I don't.	No, Idon't.
3.	firstname	first name
4.	last name	lastname
5.	NOSWIMMING	NO SWIMMING
6.	Don't walk.	Don'twalk.
7.	NO SMOKING	NOSMOKING

B. Trace.

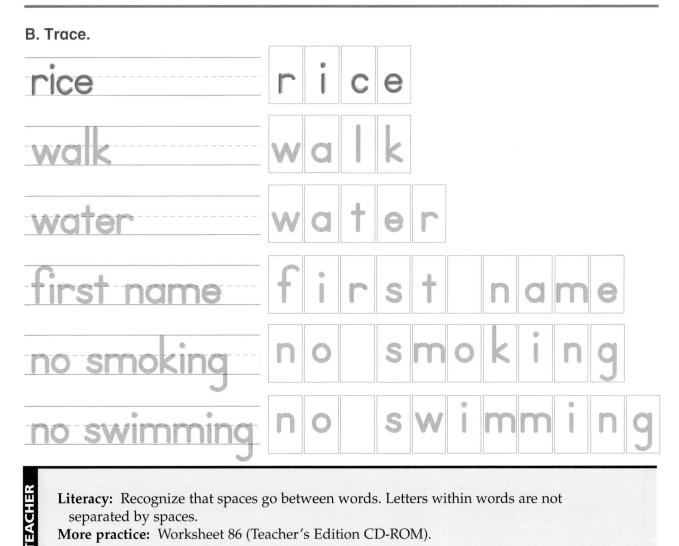

rice   r i c e

walk   w a l k

water   w a t e r

first name   f i r s t   n a m e

no smoking   n o   s m o k i n g

no swimming   n o   s w i m m i n g

TEACHER

Literacy: Recognize that spaces go between words. Letters within words are not separated by spaces.
More practice: Worksheet 86 (Teacher's Edition CD-ROM).

A. Look.

J	E	N		P	R	A	T	T							

NAME

B. Write your name.

NAME

C. Look.

Jen   Pratt

FIRST NAME   LAST NAME

D. Write your name.

FIRST NAME   LAST NAME

E. Write your name.

LAST NAME   FIRST NAME

🎧 A. Look and listen.

1.　　　　　　　2.　　　　　　　3.

4.　　　　　　　5.　　　　　　　6.

🎧 B. Listen again and repeat.

🎧 C. Listen and circle.

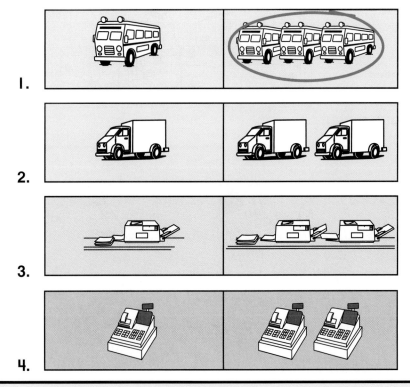

1.

2.

3.

4.

TEACHER

Survival: Learn singular and plural forms of machines, vehicles, and equipment.
New language: A truck, trucks / a car, cars / a copier, copiers / a lawn mower, lawn mowers / a cash register, cash registers / a bus, buses.

🎧 **A. Look, listen, and read.**

1.

🎧 **B. Listen again and repeat.**

🎧 **C. Look and listen.**

🎧 **D. Listen again and repeat.**

E. Pair work.

TEACHER

Survival: Answer interview questions about technology skills.

Civics concept: Employers ask about ability to use machines and equipment.

New language: Can you use a [cash register]? / Can you drive a [car]? / Yes, I can. / No, I can't. / What skills do you have?

Circle.

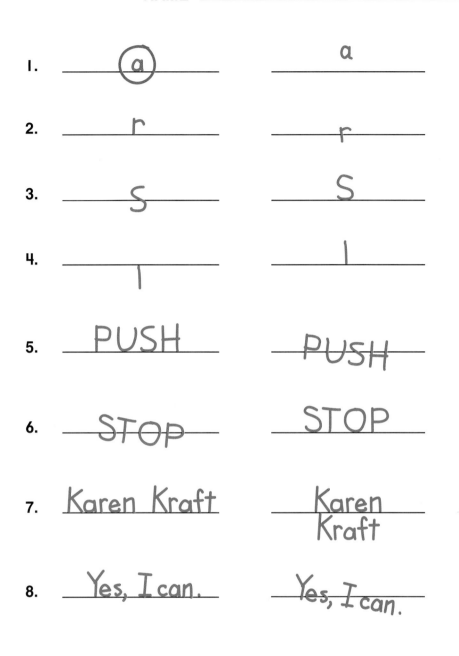

1. (a)   a

2. r   r

3. S   S

4. | |

5. PUSH   ~~PUSH~~

6. ~~STOP~~   STOP

7. Karen Kraft   Karen
                  Kraft

8. Yes, I can.   Yes, I can.

TEACHER

Literacy: Recognize letters and words written correctly on the line.

A. Write lowercase letters.

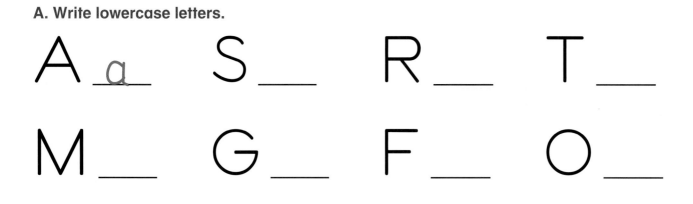

A a   S _   R _ _   T _

M _ _   G _ _   F _ _   O _ _

B. Write capital letters.

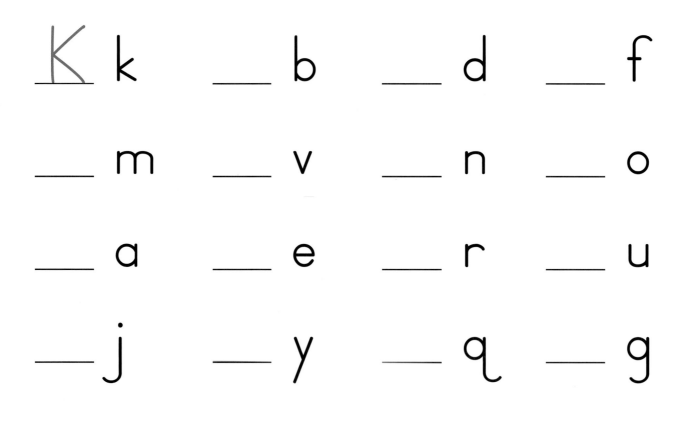

K k   _ b   _ d   _ f

_ m   _ v   _ n   _ o

_ a   _ e   _ r   _ u

_ j   _ y   _ q   _ g

🎧 A. Look, listen, and read.

🎧 B. Listen again and repeat.

🎧 C. Look, listen, and read.

1.

2.

🎧 D. Listen again and repeat.

E. Pair work.

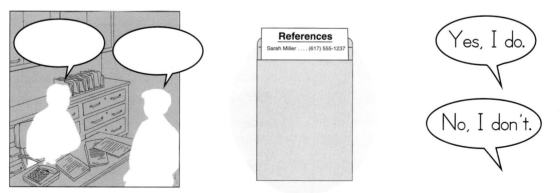

References
Sarah Miller . . . . (617) 555-1237

A. Listen and write the last name.

APPLICATION

L O U I S A □ □ □ □ □

Name

H O U S E K E E P E R

Occupation

B. Look and listen.

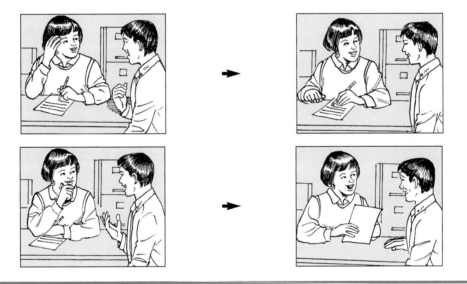

C. Listen and respond.

1.   2.   3.

A. Look.

B. Write <u>your</u> name and phone number.

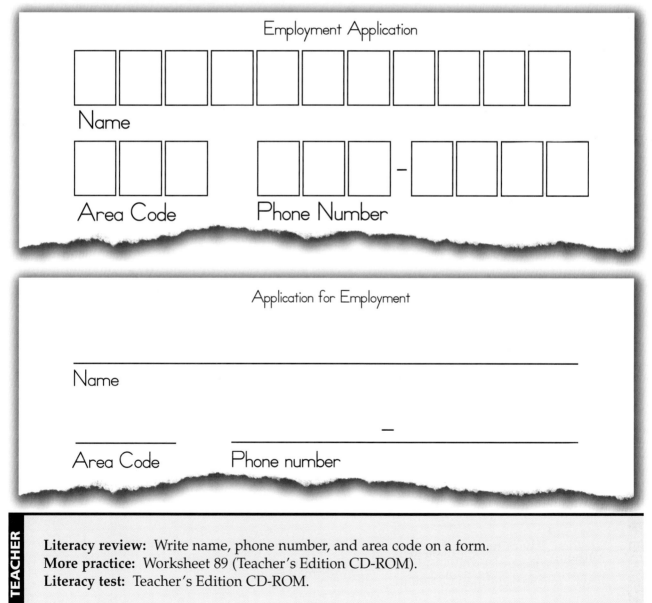

Talk about the pictures. Role-play conversations.

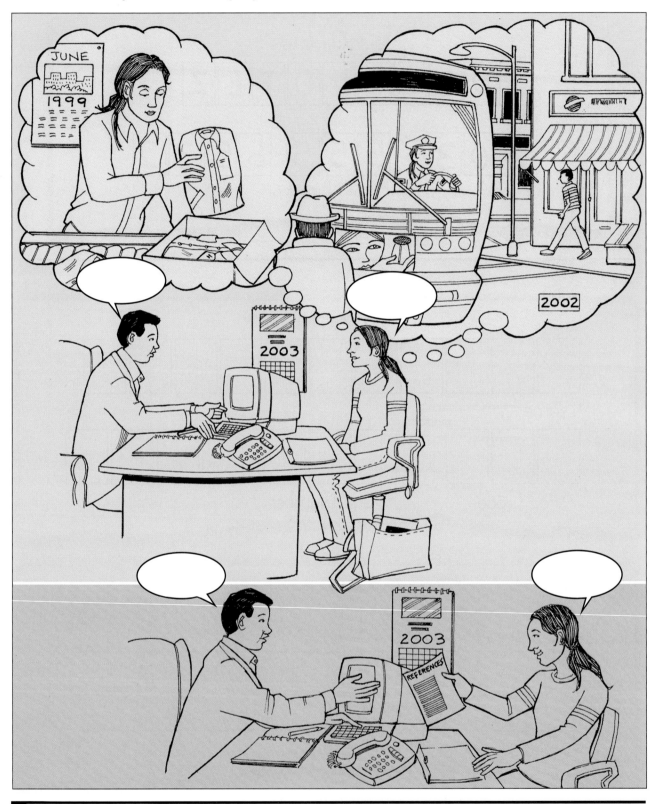

TEACHER

Survival / civics review: Point and name things in the pictures. Make statements about the pictures. Role-play conversations based on the pictures.

Tests: Teacher's Edition CD-ROM.